# THE BAR SINISTER

Miss Dorothy snatches me up and kisses me
between the ears.

# THE NOVELS AND STORIES OF RICHARD HARDING DAVIS

# THE BAR SINISTER

BY

## RICHARD HARDING DAVIS

WITH AN INTRODUCTION BY

### WINSTON CHURCHILL

ILLUSTRATED

NEW YORK

CHARLES SCRIBNER'S SONS

1918

# RICHARD HARDING DAVIS

On that day when I read of Mr. Davis's sudden death, there came back to me a vivid memory of another day, some eighteen years ago, when I first met him, shortly after the publication of my first novel. I was paying an over-Sunday visit to Marion, that quaint waterside resort where Mr. Davis lived for many years, and with which his name is associated. On the Monday morning, as the stage started out for the station, a young man came running after it, caught it, and sat down in the only empty place—beside me. He was Richard Harding Davis. I recognized him, nor shall I forget that peculiar thrill I experienced at finding myself in actual, physical contact with an author. And that this author should be none other than the creator of Gallegher, prepossessing, vigorous, rather than a dry and elderly recluse, made my excitement the keener. It happened also, after entering the smoking-car, that the remaining vacant seat was at my side, and here Mr. Davis established himself. He looked at me, he asked if my name was Winston Churchill, he said he had read my book. How he guessed my identity I did not discover. But the recollection of our talk, the strong impression I then received of Mr. Davis's vitality and personality, the liking I conceived for him—these have neither changed nor faded with the years, and I recall with gratitude to-day the kindliness, the sense of fellowship always so strong in him that impelled him to speak as he did. A month before he died, when I met him on the train going to Mt. Kisco, he had not changed. His enthusiasms, his vigor, his fine passions, his fondness for his friends, these, nor the joy he found in the pursuit of his profession, had not faded. And there come to me now, as I think of him filled with life, flashes from his writings that have moved me, and move me indescribably still. "*Le Style*," as Rolland remarks, "*c'est l'âme.*" It was so in Mr. Davis's case. He had the rare faculty of stirring by a phrase the imaginations of men, of including in a phrase a picture, an event—a cataclysm. Such a phrase was that in which he described the entry of German hosts into Brussels. He was not a man, when enlisted in a cause, to count the cost to himself. Many causes will miss him, and many friends, and many admirers, yet his personality remains with us forever, in his work.

WINSTON CHURCHILL.

# CONTENTS

# ILLUSTRATIONS

# THE BAR SINISTER

# PREFACE

When this story first appeared, the writer received letters of two kinds, one asking a question and the other making a statement. The question was, whether there was any foundation of truth in the story; the statement challenged him to say that there was. The letters seemed to show that a large proportion of readers prefer their dose of fiction with a sweetening of fact. This is written to furnish that condiment, and to answer the question and the statement.

In the dog world, the original of the bull-terrier in the story is known as Edgewood Cold Steel and to his intimates as "Kid." His father was Lord Minto, a thoroughbred bull-terrier, well known in Canada, but the story of Kid's life is that his mother was a black-and-tan named Vic. She was a lady of doubtful pedigree. Among her offspring by Lord Minto, so I have been often informed by many Canadian dog-fanciers, breeders, and exhibitors, was the only white puppy, Kid, in a litter of black-and-tans. He made his first appearance in the show world in 1900 in Toronto, where, under the judging of Mr. Charles H. Mason, he was easily first. During that year, when he came to our kennels, and in the two years following, he carried off many blue ribbons and cups at nearly every first-class show in the country. The other dog, "Jimmy Jocks," who in the book was his friend and mentor, was in real life his friend and companion, Woodcote Jumbo, or "Jaggers," an aristocratic son of a long line of English champions. He has gone to that place where some day all good dogs must go.

In this autobiography I have tried to describe Kid as he really is, and this year, when he again strives for blue ribbons, I trust, should the gentle reader see him at any of the bench-shows, he will give him a friendly pat and make his acquaintance. He will find his advances met with a polite and gentle courtesy.

The Author.

# THE BAR SINISTER

## PART I

THE Master was walking most unsteady, his legs tripping each other. After the fifth or sixth round, my legs often go the same way.

But even when the Master's legs bend and twist a bit, you mustn't think he can't reach you. Indeed, that is the time he kicks most frequent. So I kept behind him in the shadow, or ran in the middle of the street. He stopped at many public-houses with swinging doors, those doors that are cut so high from the sidewalk that you can look in under them, and see if the Master is inside. At night when I peep beneath them the man at the counter will see me first and say, "Here's the Kid, Jerry, come to take you home. Get a move on you," and the Master will stumble out and follow me. It's lucky for us I'm so white, for no matter how dark the night, he can always see me ahead, just out of reach of his boot. At night the Master certainly does see most amazing. Sometimes he sees two or four of me, and walks in a circle, so that I have to take him by the leg of

3

his trousers and lead him into the right road. One night, when he was very nasty-tempered and I was coaxing him along, two men passed us and one of them says, "Look at that brute!" and the other asks "Which?" and they both laugh. The Master, he cursed them good and proper.

This night, whenever we stopped at a public-house, the Master's pals left it and went on with us to the next. They spoke quite civil to me, and when the Master tried a flying kick, they gives him a shove. "Do you want we should lose our money?" says the pals.

I had had nothing to eat for a day and a night, and just before we set out the Master gives me a wash under the hydrant. Whenever I am locked up until all the slop-pans in our alley are empty, and made to take a bath, and the Master's pals speak civil, and feel my ribs, I know something is going to happen. And that night, when every time they see a policeman under a lamp-post, they dodged across the street, and when at the last one of them picked me up and hid me under his jacket, I began to tremble; for I knew what it meant. It meant that I was to fight again for the Master.

I don't fight because I like it. I fight because if I didn't the other dog would find my throat, and the Master would lose his stakes, and I would be very sorry for him and ashamed. Dogs can pass me and I can pass dogs, and I'd never pick a fight with none of them. When I see two dogs standing on their hind-legs in the streets, clawing each other's ears, and snapping for each other's windpipes, or howling and swearing and rolling in the mud, I feel sorry they should act so, and pretend not to notice. If he'd let me, I'd like to pass the time of day with every dog I meet. But there's something about me that no nice dog can abide. When I trot up to nice dogs, nodding and grinning, to make friends, they always tell me to be off. "Go to the devil!" they bark at me; "Get out!" and when I walk away they shout "mongrel," and "gutter-dog," and sometimes, after my back is turned, they rush me. I could kill most of them with three shakes, breaking the back-bone of the little ones, and squeezing the throat of the big ones. But what's the good? They *are* nice dogs; that's why I try to make up to them, and though it's not for them to say it, I *am* a street-dog, and if I try to push into the company of my betters, I suppose it's their right to teach me my place.

Of course, they don't know I'm the best fighting bull-terrier of my weight in Montreal. That's why it wouldn't be right for me to take

no notice of what they shout. They don't
know that if I once locked my jaws on them
I'd carry away whatever I touched. The night
I fought Kelley's White Rat, I wouldn't loosen
up until the Master made a noose in my leash
and strangled me, and if the handlers hadn't
thrown red pepper down my nose, I *never* would
have let go of that Ottawa dog. I don't think
the handlers treated me quite right that time,
but maybe they didn't know the Ottawa dog
was dead. I did.

I learned my fighting from my mother when I
was very young. We slept in a lumber-yard on
the river-front, and by day hunted for food along
the wharfs. When we got it, the other tramp-
dogs would try to take it off us, and then it was
wonderful to see mother fly at them, and drive
them away. All I know of fighting I learned
from mother, watching her picking the ash-
heaps for me when I was too little to fight for
myself. No one ever was so good to me as
mother. When it snowed and the ice was in
the St. Lawrence she used to hunt alone, and
bring me back new bones, and she'd sit and
laugh to see me trying to swallow 'em whole.
I was just a puppy then, my teeth was falling
out. When I was able to fight we kept the
whole river-range to ourselves. I had the
genuine long, "punishing" jaw, so mother said,

and there wasn't a man or a dog that dared worry us. Those were happy days, those were; and we lived well, share and share alike, and when we wanted a bit of fun, we chased the fat old wharf-rats. My! how they would squeal!

Then the trouble came. It was no trouble to me. I was too young to care then. But mother took it so to heart that she grew ailing, and wouldn't go abroad with me by day. It was the same old scandal that they're always bringing up against me. I was so young then that I didn't know. I couldn't see any difference between mother—and other mothers.

But one day a pack of curs we drove off snarled back some new names at her, and mother dropped her head and ran, just as though they had whipped us. After that she wouldn't go out with me except in the dark, and one day she went away and never came back, and though I hunted for her in every court and alley and back street of Montreal, I never found her.

One night, a month after mother ran away, I asked Guardian, the old blind mastiff, whose Master is the night-watchman on our slip, what it all meant. And he told me.

"Every dog in Montreal knows," he says, "except you, and every Master knows. So I think it's time you knew."

Then he tells me that my father, who had treated mother so bad, was a great and noble gentleman from London. "Your father had twenty-two registered ancestors, had your father," old Guardian says, "and in him was the best bull-terrier blood of England, the most ancientest, the most royal; the winning 'blue-ribbon' blood, that breeds champions. He had sleepy pink eyes, and thin pink lips, and he was as white all over as his own white teeth, and under his white skin you could see his muscles, hard and smooth, like the links of a steel chain. When your father stood still, and tipped his nose in the air, it was just as though he was saying, 'Oh, yes, you common dogs and men, you may well stare. It must be a rare treat for you Colonials to see a real English royalty.' He certainly was pleased with hisself, was your father. He looked just as proud and haughty as one of them stone dogs in Victoria Park— them as is cut out of white marble. And you're like him," says the old mastiff—"by that, of course, meaning you're white, same as him. That's the only likeness. But, you see, the trouble is, Kid—well, you see, Kid, the trouble is—your mother——"

"That will do," I said, for I understood then without his telling me, and I got up and walked away, holding my head and tail high in the air.

But I was, oh, so miserable, and I wanted to see mother that very minute, and tell her that I didn't care.

Mother is what I am, a street-dog; there's no royal blood in mother's veins, nor is she like that father of mine, nor—and that's the worst—she's not even like me. For while I, when I'm washed for a fight, am as white as clean snow, she—and this is our trouble, she—my mother, is a black-and-tan.

When mother hid herself from me, I was twelve months old and able to take care of myself, and, as after mother left me, the wharfs were never the same, I moved up-town and met the Master. Before he came, lots of other men-folks had tried to make up to me, and to whistle me home. But they either tried patting me or coaxing me with a piece of meat; so I didn't take to 'em. But one day the Master pulled me out of a street-fight by the hind-legs, and kicked me good.

"You want to fight, do you?" says he. "I'll give you all the *fighting* you want!" he says, and he kicks me again. So I knew he was my Master, and I followed him home. Since that day I've pulled off many fights for him, and they've brought dogs from all over the province to have a go at me, but up to that night none under thirty pounds, had ever downed me.

But that night, so soon as they carried me into the ring, I saw the dog was over-weight, and that I was no match for him. It was asking too much of a puppy. The Master should have known I couldn't do it. Not that I mean to blame the Master, for when sober, which he sometimes was, though not, as you might say, his habit, he was most kind to me, and let me out to find food, if I could get it, and only kicked me when I didn't pick him up at night and lead him home.

But kicks will stiffen the muscles, and starving a dog so as to get him ugly-tempered for a fight may make him nasty, but it's weakening to his insides, and it causes the legs to wabble.

The ring was in a hall, back of a public-house. There was a red-hot whitewashed stove in one corner, and the ring in the other. I lay in the Master's lap, wrapped in my blanket, and, spite of the stove, shivering awful; but I always shiver before a fight; I can't help gettin' excited. While the men-folks were a-flashing their money and taking their last drink at the bar, a little Irish groom in gaiters came up to me and give me the back of his hand to smell, and scratched me behind the ears.

"You poor little pup," says he. "You haven't no show," he says. "That brute in the tap-room, he'll eat your heart out."

"That's what you think," says the Master, snarling. "I'll lay you a quid the Kid chews him up."

The groom, he shook his head, but kept looking at me so sorry-like, that I begun to get a bit sad myself. He seemed like he couldn't bear to leave off a-patting of me, and he says, speaking low just like he would to a man-folk, "Well, good-luck to you, little pup," which I thought so civil of him, that I reached up and licked his hand. I don't do that to many men. And the Master, he knew I didn't, and took on dreadful.

"What 'ave you got on the back of your hand?" says he, jumping up.

"Soap!" says the groom, quick as a rat. "That's more than you've got on yours. Do you want to smell of it?" and he sticks his fist under the Master's nose. But the pals pushed in between 'em.

"He tried to poison the Kid!" shouts the Master.

"Oh, one fight at a time," says the referee. "Get into the ring, Jerry. We're waiting." So we went into the ring.

I never could just remember what did happen in that ring. He give me no time to spring. He fell on me like a horse. I couldn't keep my feet against him, and though, as I saw, he could get his hold when he liked, he wanted to chew me over a bit first. I was wondering if they'd be able to pry him off me, when, in the third round, he took his hold; and I began to drown, just as I did when I fell into the river off the Red C slip. He closed deeper and deeper, on my throat, and everything went black and red and bursting; and then, when I were sure I were dead, the handlers pulled him off, and the Master give me a kick that brought me to. But I couldn't move none, or even wink, both eyes being shut with lumps.

"He's a cur!" yells the Master, "a sneaking, cowardly cur. He lost the fight for me," says he, "because he's a —— —— —— cowardly cur." And he kicks me again in the lower ribs, so that I go sliding across the sawdust. "There's gratitude fer yer," yells the Master. "I've fed that dog, and nussed that dog, and housed him like a prince; and now he puts his tail between his legs, and sells me out, he does. He's a coward; I've done with him, I am. I'd sell him for a pipeful of tobacco." He picked me up by the tail, and swung me for the men-folks to see. "Does any gentleman here want to buy a dog," he says, "to make into sausage meat?" he says. "That's all he's good for."

Then I heard the little Irish groom say, "I'll give you ten bob for the dog."

And another voice says, "Ah, don't you do it; the dog's same as dead—mebby he is dead."

"Ten shillings!" says the Master, and his voice sobers a bit; "make it two pounds, and he's yours."

But the pals rushed in again.

"Don't you be a fool, Jerry," they say. "You'll be sorry for this when you're sober. The Kid's worth a fiver."

One of my eyes was not so swelled up as the other, and as I hung by my tail, I opened it, and saw one of the pals take the groom by the shoulder.

"You ought to give 'im five pounds for that dog, mate," he says; "that's no ordinary dog. That dog's got good blood in him, that dog has. Why, his father—that very dog's father——"

I thought he never would go on. He waited like he wanted to be sure the groom was listening.

"That very dog's father," says the pal, "is Regent Royal, son of Champion Regent Monarch, champion bull-terrier of England for four years."

I was sore, and torn, and chewed most awful, but what the pal said sounded so fine that I wanted to wag my tail, only couldn't, owing to my hanging from it.

But the Master calls out, "Yes, his father was Regent Royal; who's saying he wasn't? but the pup's a cowardly cur, that's what his pup is, and why—I'll tell you why—because his mother was a black-and-tan street-dog, that's why!"

I don't see how I get the strength, but some way I threw myself out of the Master's grip and fell at his feet, and turned over and fastened all my teeth in his ankle, just across the bone.

When I woke, after the pals had kicked me off him, I was in the smoking-car of a railroad-train, lying in the lap of the little groom, and he was rubbing my open wounds with a greasy, yellow stuff, exquisite to the smell, and most agreeable to lick off.

# PART II

"WELL—what's your name—Nolan? Well,
Nolan, these references are satisfactory," said
the young gentleman my new Master called
"Mr. Wyndham, sir." "I'll take you on as
second man. You can begin to-day."

My new Master shuffled his feet, and put his
finger to his forehead. "Thank you, sir," says
he. Then he choked like he had swallowed a
fish-bone. "I have a little dawg, sir," says he.

"You can't keep him," says "Mr. Wyndham,
sir," very short.

"'Es only a puppy, sir," says my new Master;
"'e wouldn't go outside the stables, sir."

"It's not that," says "Mr. Wyndham, sir";
"I have a large kennel of very fine dogs; they're
the best of their breed in America. I don't
allow strange dogs on the premises."

The Master shakes his head, and motions me
with his cap, and I crept out from behind the
door. "I'm sorry, sir," says the Master. "Then
I can't take the place. I can't get along without
the dog, sir."

"Mr. Wyndham, sir," looked at me that fierce
that I guessed he was going to whip me, so I

turned over on my back and begged with my legs and tail.

"Why, you beat him!" says "Mr. Wyndham, sir," very stern.

"No fear!" the Master says, getting very red. "The party I bought him off taught him that. He never learnt that from me!" He picked me up in his arms, and to show "Mr. Wyndham, sir," how well I loved the Master, I bit his chin and hands.

"Mr. Wyndham, sir," turned over the letters the Master had given him. "Well, these references certainly are very strong," he says. "I guess I'll let the dog stay this time. Only see you keep him away from the kennels—or you'll both go."

"Thank you, sir," says the Master, grinning like a cat when she's safe behind the area-railing.

"He's not a bad bull-terrier," says "Mr. Wyndham, sir," feeling my head. "Not that I know much about the smooth-coated breeds. My dogs are St. Bernards." He stopped patting me and held up my nose. "What's the matter with his ears?" he says. "They're chewed to pieces. Is this a fighting dog?" he asks, quick and rough-like.

I could have laughed. If he hadn't been holding my nose, I certainly would have had a good grin at him. Me, the best under thirty pounds in the Province of Quebec, and him asking if I was a fighting dog! I ran to the Master and hung down my head modest-like, waiting for him to tell of my list of battles, but the Master he coughs in his cap most painful. "Fightin' dog, sir," he cries. "Lor' bless you, sir, the Kid don't know the word. 'Es just a puppy, sir, same as you see; a pet dog, so to speak. 'Es a regular old lady's lap-dog, the Kid is."

"Well, you keep him away from my St. Bernards," says "Mr. Wyndham, sir," "or they might make a mouthful of him."

"Yes, sir, that they might," says the Master. But when we gets outside he slaps his knee and laughs inside hisself, and winks at me most sociable.

The Master's new home was in the country, in a province they called Long Island. There was a high stone wall about his home with big iron gates to it, same as Godfrey's brewery; and there was a house with five red roofs, and the stables, where I lived, was cleaner than the aerated bakery-shop, and then there was the kennels, but they was like nothing else in this world that ever I see. For the first days I couldn't sleep of nights for fear some one would catch me lying in such a cleaned-up place, and

would chase me out of it, and when I did fall
to sleep I'd dream I was back in the old Master's
attic, shivering under the rusty stove, which
never had no coals in it, with the Master flat on
his back on the cold floor with his clothes on.
And I'd wake up, scared and whimpering, and
find myself on the new Master's cot with his
hand on the quilt beside me; and I'd see the
glow of the big stove, and hear the high-quality
horses below-stairs stamping in their straw-
lined boxes, and I'd snoop the sweet smell of
hay and harness-soap, and go to sleep again.

The stables was my jail, so the Master said,
but I don't ask no better home than that jail.

"Now, Kid," says he, sitting on the top of a
bucket upside down, "you've got to understand
this. When I whistle it means you're not to go
out of this 'ere yard. These stables is your
jail. And if you leave 'em I'll have to leave
'em, too, and over the seas, in the County Mayo,
an old mother will 'ave to leave her bit of a
cottage. For two pounds I must be sending
her every month, or she'll have naught to eat,
nor no thatch over 'er head; so, I can't lose my
place, Kid, an' see you don't lose it for me.
You must keep away from the kennels," says
he; "they're not for the likes of you. The
kennels are for the quality. I wouldn't take a
litter of them woolly dogs for one wag of your

tail, Kid, but for all that they are your betters,
same as the gentry up in the big house are my
betters. I know my place and keep away from
the gentry, and you keep away from the champions."

So I never goes out of the stables. All day
I just lay in the sun on the stone flags, licking
my jaws, and watching the grooms wash down
the carriages, and the only care I had was to
see they didn't get gay and turn the hose on
me. There wasn't even a single rat to plague
me. Such stables I never did see.

"Nolan," says the head-groom, "some day
that dog of yours will give you the slip. You
can't keep a street-dog tied up all his life. It's
against his natur'." The head-groom is a nice
old gentleman, but he doesn't know everything.
Just as though I'd been a street-dog because I
liked it. As if I'd rather poke for my vittels
in ash-heaps than have 'em handed me in a
wash-basin and would sooner bite and fight
than be polite and sociable. If I'd had mother
there I couldn't have asked for nothing more.
But I'd think of her snooping in the gutters, or
freezing of nights under the bridges, or, what's
worse of all, running through the hot streets
with her tongue down, so wild and crazy for a
drink, that the people would shout "mad dog"
at her, and stone her. Water's so good, that I

don't blame the men-folks for locking it up inside their houses, but when the hot days come, I think they might remember that those are the dog-days and leave a little water outside in a trough, like they do for the horses. Then we wouldn't go mad, and the policemen wouldn't shoot us. I had so much of everything I wanted that it made me think a lot of the days when I hadn't nothing, and if I could have given what I had to mother, as she used to share with me, I'd have been the happiest dog in the land. Not that I wasn't happy then, and most grateful to the Master, too, and if I'd only minded him, the trouble wouldn't have come again.

But one day the coachman says that the little lady they called Miss Dorothy had come back from school, and that same morning she runs over to the stables to pat her ponies, and she sees me.

"Oh, what a nice little, white little dog," said she; "whose little dog are you?" says she.

"That's my dog, miss," says the Master. "'Is name is Kid," and I ran up to her most polite, and licks her fingers, for I never see so pretty and kind a lady.

"You must come with me and call on my new puppies," says she, picking me up in her arms and starting off with me.

"Oh, but please, miss," cries Nolan, "Mr. Wyndham give orders that the Kid's not to go to the kennels."

"That'll be all right," says the little lady; "they're my kennels too. And the puppies will like to play with him."

You wouldn't believe me if I was to tell you of the style of them quality-dogs. If I hadn't seen it myself I wouldn't have believed it neither. The Viceroy of Canada don't live no better. There was forty of them, but each one had his own house and a yard—most exclusive —and a cot and a drinking-basin all to hisself. They had servants standing 'round waiting to feed 'em when they was hungry, and valets to wash 'em; and they had their hair combed and brushed like the grooms must when they go out on the box. Even the puppies had overcoats with their names on 'em in blue letters, and the name of each of those they called champions was painted up fine over his front door just like it was a public-house or a veterinary's. They were the biggest St. Bernards I ever did see. I could have walked under them if they'd have let me. But they were very proud and haughty dogs, and looked only once at me, and then sniffed in the air. The little lady's own dog was an old gentleman bull-dog. He'd come along with us, and when he notices how taken aback I was with all I see, 'e turned quite kind and affable and showed me about.

"Jimmy Jocks," Miss Dorothy called him, but, owing to his weight, he walked most dignified and slow, waddling like a duck as you might say, and looked much too proud and handsome for such a silly name.

"That's the runway, and that's the Trophy House," says he to me, "and that over there is the hospital, where you have to go if you get distemper, and the vet. gives you beastly medicine."

"And which of these is your 'ouse, sir?" asks I, wishing to be respectful. But he looked that hurt and haughty. "I don't live in the kennels," says he, most contemptuous. "I am a house-dog. I sleep in Miss Dorothy's room. And at lunch I'm let in with the family, if the visitors don't mind. They most always do, but they're too polite to say so. Besides," says he, smiling most condescending, "visitors are always afraid of me. It's because I'm so ugly," says he. "I suppose," says he, screwing up his wrinkles and speaking very slow and impressive, "I suppose I'm the ugliest bull-dog in America," and as he seemed to be so pleased to think hisself so, I said, "Yes, sir, you certainly are the ugliest ever I see," at which he nodded his head most approving.

"I suppose I'm the ugliest bull-dog in America."

"But I couldn't hurt 'em, as you say," he goes on, though I hadn't said nothing like that, being too polite. "I'm too old," he says; "I haven't any teeth. The last time one of those grizzly bears," said he, glaring at the big St. Bernards, "took a hold of me, he nearly was my death," says he. I thought his eyes would pop out of his head, he seemed so wrought up about it. "He rolled me around in the dirt, he did," says Jimmy Jocks, "an' I couldn't get up. It was low," says Jimmy Jocks, making a face like he had a bad taste in his mouth. "Low, that's what I call it, bad form, you understand, young man, not done in our circles—and—and low." He growled, way down in his stomach, and puffed hisself out, panting and blowing like he had been on a run.

"I'm not a street-fighter," he says, scowling at a St. Bernard marked "Champion." "And when my rheumatism is not troubling me," he says, "I endeavor to be civil to all dogs, so long as they are gentlemen."

"Yes, sir," said I, for even to me he had been most affable.

At this we had come to a little house off by itself and Jimmy Jocks invites me in. "This is their trophy-room," he says, "where they keep their prizes. Mine," he says, rather grand-like, "are on the sideboard." Not knowing what a sideboard might be, I said, "Indeed, sir, that must be very gratifying." But he only wrinkled up his chops as much as to say, "It is my right."

The trophy-room was as wonderful as any public-house I ever see. On the walls was pictures of nothing but beautiful St. Bernard dogs, and rows and rows of blue and red and yellow ribbons; and when I asked Jimmy Jocks why they was so many more of blue than of the others, he laughs and says, "Because these kennels always win." And there was many shining cups on the shelves which Jimmy Jocks told me were prizes won by the champions

"Now, sir, might I ask you, sir," says I, "wot is a champion?"

At that he panted and breathed so hard I thought he would bust hisself. "My dear young friend!" says he. "Wherever have you been educated? A champion is a—a champion," he says. "He must win nine blue ribbons in the 'open' class. You follow me—that is—against all comers. Then he has the title before his name, and they put his photograph in the sporting papers. You know, of course, that *I* am a champion," says he. "I am Champion Woodstock Wizard III., and the two other Woodstock Wizards, my father and uncle, were both champions."

"But I thought your name was Jimmy Jocks," I said.

He laughs right out at that.

"That's my kennel name, not my registered name," he says. "Why, you certainly know that every dog has two names. Now, what's your registered name and number, for instance?" says he.

"I've only got one name," I says. "Just Kid."

Woodstock Wizard puffs at that and wrinkles up his forehead and pops out his eyes.

"Who are your people?" says he. "Where is your home?"

"At the stable, sir," I said. "My Master is the second groom."

At that Woodstock Wizard III looks at me for quite a bit without winking, and stares all around the room over my head.

"Oh, well," says he at last, "you're a very civil young dog," says he, "and I blame no one for what he can't help," which I thought most fair and liberal. "And I have known many bull-terriers that were champions," says he, "though as a rule they mostly run with fire-engines, and to fighting. For me, I wouldn't care to run through the streets after a hose-cart, nor to fight," says he; "but each to his taste."

I could not help thinking that if Woodstock

25

Wizard III tried to follow a fire-engine he would
die of apoplexy, and that, seeing he'd lost his
teeth, it was lucky he had no taste for fighting,
but, after his being so condescending, I didn't
say nothing.

"Anyway," says he, "every smooth-coated
dog is better than any hairy old camel like those
St. Bernards, and if ever you're hungry down at
the stables, young man, come up to the house
and I'll give you a bone. I can't eat them
myself, but I bury them around the garden from
force of habit, and in case a friend should drop
in. Ah, I see my Mistress coming," he says,
"and I bid you good-day. I regret," he says,
"that our different social position prevents our
meeting frequent, for you're a worthy young
dog with a proper respect for your betters, and
in this country there's precious few of them
have that." Then he waddles off, leaving me
alone and very sad, for he was the first dog
in many days that had spoken to me. But
since he showed, seeing that I was a stable-
dog, he didn't want my company, I waited for
him to get well away. It was not a cheerful
place to wait, the Trophy House. The pictures
of the champions seemed to scowl at me, and
ask what right had such as I even to admire
them, and the blue and gold ribbons and the
silver cups made me very miserable. I had

never won no blue ribbons or silver cups; only
stakes for the old Master to spend in the publics,
and I hadn't won them for being a beautiful,
high-quality dog, but just for fighting—which,
of course, as Woodstock Wizard III says, is
low. So I started for the stables, with my head
down and my tail between my legs, feeling
sorry I had ever left the Master. But I had
more reason to be sorry before I got back to him.

The Trophy House was quite a bit from the
kennels, and as I left it I see Miss Dorothy and
Woodstock Wizard III walking back toward
them, and that a fine, big St. Bernard, his name
was Champion Red Elfberg, had broke his chain,
and was running their way. When he reaches
old Jimmy Jocks he lets out a roar like a
grain-steamer in a fog, and he makes three leaps
for him. Old Jimmy Jocks was about a fourth
his size; but he plants his feet and curves his
back, and his hair goes up around his neck like
a collar. But he never had no show at no time,
for the grizzly bear, as Jimmy Jocks had called
him, lights on old Jimmy's back and tries to
break it, and old Jimmy Jocks snaps his gums
and claws the grass, panting and groaning
awful. But he can't do nothing, and the
grizzly bear just rolls him under him, biting and
tearing cruel. The odds was all that Woodstock
Wizard III was going to be killed. I had

fought enough to see that, but not knowing
the rules of the game among champions, I
didn't like to interfere between two gentlemen
who might be settling a private affair, and, as
it were, take it as presuming of me. So I stood
by, though I was shaking terrible, and holding
myself in like I was on a leash. But at that
Woodstock Wizard III, who was underneath,
sees me through the dust, and calls very faint,
"Help, you!" he says. "Take him in the hind-
leg," he says. "He's murdering me," he says.
And then the little Miss Dorothy, who was
crying, and calling to the kennel-men, catches
at the Red Elfberg's hind-legs to pull him off,
and the brute, keeping his front pats well in
Jimmy's stomach, turns his big head and snaps
at her. So that was all I asked for, thank you.
I went up under him. It was really nothing.
He stood so high that I had only to take off
about three feet from him and come in from the
side, and my long, "punishing jaw" as mother
was always talking about, locked on his woolly
throat, and my back teeth met. I couldn't
shake him, but I shook myself, and every time
I shook myself there was thirty pounds of
weight tore at his windpipes. I couldn't see
nothing for his long hair, but I heard Jimmy
Jocks puffing and blowing on one side, and
munching the brute's leg with his old gums.

Jimmy was an old sport that day, was Jimmy, or, Woodstock Wizard III., as I should say. When the Red Elfberg was out and down I had to run, or those kennel-men would have had my life. They chased me right into the stables; and from under the hay I watched the head-groom take down a carriage-whip and order them to the right about. Luckily Master and the young grooms were out, or that day there'd have been fighting for everybody.

Well, it nearly did for me and the Master. "Mr. Wyndham, sir," comes raging to the stables and said I'd half-killed his best prize-winner, and had oughter be shot, and he gives the Master his notice. But Miss Dorothy she follows him, and says it was his Red Elfberg what began the fight, and that I'd saved Jimmy's life, and that old Jimmy Jocks was worth more to her than all the St. Bernards in the Swiss mountains—wherever they be. And that I was her champion, anyway. Then she cried over me most beautiful, and over Jimmy Jocks, too, who was that tied up in bandages he couldn't even waddle. So when he heard that side of it, "Mr. Wyndham, sir," told us that if Nolan put me on a chain, we could stay. So it came out all right for everybody but me. I was glad the Master kept his place, but I'd never worn a chain before, and it disheartened me—but that was the least of it. For the quality-dogs couldn't forgive my whipping their champion, and they came to the fence between the kennels and the stables, and laughed through the bars, barking most cruel words at me. I couldn't understand how they found it out, but they knew. After the fight Jimmy Jocks was most condescending to me, and he said the grooms had boasted to the kennel-men that I was a son of Regent Royal, and that when the kennel-men asked who was my mother they had had to tell them that too. Perhaps that was the way of it, but, however, the scandal was out, and every one of the quality-dogs knew that I was a street-dog and the son of a black-and-tan.

"These misalliances will occur," said Jimmy Jocks, in his old-fashioned way, "but no well-bred dog," says he, looking most scornful at the St. Bernards, who were howling behind the palings, "would refer to your misfortune before you, certainly not cast it in your face. I, myself, remember your father's father, when he made his début at the Crystal Palace. He took four blue ribbons and three specials."

But no sooner than Jimmy would leave me, the St. Bernards would take to howling again, insulting mother and insulting me. And when I tore at my chain, they, seeing they were safe,

would howl the more. It was never the same
after that; the laughs and the jeers cut into my
heart, and the chain bore heavy on my spirit.
I was so sad that sometimes I wished I was back
in the gutter again, where no one was better
than me, and some nights I wished I was dead.
If it hadn't been for the Master being so kind,
and that it would have looked like I was blaming
mother, I would have twisted my leash and
hanged myself.

About a month after my fight, the word was
passed through the kennels that the New York
Show was coming, and such goings on as followed I never did see. If each of them had been
matched to fight for a thousand pounds and the
gate, they couldn't have trained more conscien-
tious. But, perhaps, that's just my envy. The
kennel-men rubbed 'em and scrubbed 'em and
trims their hair and curls and combs it, and some
dogs they fatted, and some they starved. No
one talked of nothing but the Show, and the
chances "our kennels" had against the other
kennels, and if this one of our champions would
win over that one, and whether them as hoped
to be champions had better show in the "open"
or the "limit" class, and whether this dog would
beat his own dad, or whether his little puppy
sister couldn't beat the two of them. Even the
grooms had their money up, and day or night

you heard nothing but praises of "our" dogs, until I, being so far out of it, couldn't have felt meaner if I had been running the streets with a can to my tail. I knew shows were not for such as me, and so I lay all day stretched at the end of my chain, pretending I was asleep, and only too glad that they had something so important to think of, that they could leave me alone.

But one day before the Show opened, Miss Dorothy came to the stables with "Mr. Wyndham, sir," and seeing me chained up and so miserable, she takes me in her arms.

"You poor little tyke," says she. "It's cruel to tie him up so; he's eating his heart out, Nolan," she says. "I don't know nothing about bull-terriers," says she, "but I think Kid's got good points," says she, "and you ought to show him. Jimmy Jocks has three legs on the Rensselaer Cup now, and I'm going to show him this time so that he can get the fourth, and if you wish, I'll enter your dog too. How would you like that, Kid?" says she. "How would you like to see the most beautiful dogs in the world? Maybe, you'd meet a pal or two," says she. "It would cheer you up, wouldn't it, Kid?" says she. But I was so upset, I could only wag my tail most violent. "He says it would!" says she, though, being that excited, I hadn't said nothing.

So, "Mr. Wyndham, sir," laughs and takes out a piece of blue paper, and sits down at the head-groom's table.

"What's the name of the father of your dog, Nolan?" says he. And Nolan says, "The man I got him off told me he was a son of Champion Regent Royal, sir. But it don't seem likely, does it?" says Nolan.

"It does not!" says "Mr. Wyndham, sir," short-like.

"Aren't you sure, Nolan?" says Miss Dorothy.

"No, miss," says the Master.

"Sire unknown," says "Mr. Wyndham, sir," and writes it down.

"Date of birth?" asks "Mr. Wyndham, sir."

"I—I—unknown, sir," says Nolan. And "Mr. Wyndham, sir," writes it down.

"Breeder?" says "Mr. Wyndham, sir."

"Unknown," says Nolan, getting very red around the jaws, and I drops my head and tail. And "Mr. Wyndham, sir," writes that down.

"Mother's name?" says "Mr. Wyndham, sir."

"She was a—unknown," says the Master. And I licks his hand.

"Dam unknown," says "Mr. Wyndham, sir," and writes it down. Then he takes the paper and reads out loud: "Sire unknown, dam unknown, breeder unknown, date of birth unknown. You'd better call him the 'Great Unknown,'" says he. "Who's paying his entrance-fee?"

"I am," says Miss Dorothy.

Two weeks after we all got on a train for New York; Jimmy Jocks and me following Nolan in the smoking-car, and twenty-two of the St. Bernards, in boxes and crates, and on chains and leashes. Such a barking and howling I never did hear, and when they sees me going, too, they laughs fit to kill.

"Wot is this; a circus?" says the railroad-man.

But I had no heart in it. I hated to go. I knew I was no "show" dog, even though Miss Dorothy and the Master did their best to keep me from shaming them. For before we set out Miss Dorothy brings a man from town who scrubbed and rubbed me, and sand-papered my tail, which hurt most awful, and shaved my ears with the Master's razor, so that you could most see clear through 'em, and sprinkles me over with pipe-clay, till I shines like a Tommy's cross-belts.

"Upon my word!" says Jimmy Jocks when he first sees me. "What a swell you are! You're the image of your grand-dad when he made his début at the Crystal Palace. He took four firsts and three specials." But I knew he was only trying to throw heart into me. They might scrub, and they might rub, and they might pipe-clay, but they couldn't pipe-clay the insides of me, and they was black-and-tan.

Then we came to a Garden, which it was not, but the biggest hall in the world. Inside there was lines of benches, a few miles long, and on them sat every dog in the world. If all the dog-snatchers in Montreal had worked night and day for a year, they couldn't have caught so many dogs. And they was all shouting and barking and howling so vicious, that my heart stopped beating. For at first I thought they was all enraged at my presuming to intrude, but after I got in my place, they kept at it just the same, barking at every dog as he come in; daring him to fight, and ordering him out, and asking him what breed of dog he thought he was, anyway. Jimmy Jocks was chained just behind me, and he said he never see so fine a show. "That's a hot class you're in, my lad," he says, looking over into my street, where there were thirty bull-terriers. They was all as white as cream, and each so beautiful that if I could have broke my chain, I would have run all the way home and hid myself under the horse-trough.

All night long they talked and sang, and passed greetings with old pals, and the home-sick puppies howled dismal. Them that couldn't sleep wouldn't let no others sleep, and all the electric lights burned in the roof, and in my eyes.

I could hear Jimmy Jocks snoring peaceful, but I could only doze by jerks, and when I dozed I dreamed horrible. All the dogs in the hall seemed coming at me for daring to intrude, with their jaws red and open, and their eyes blazing like the lights in the roof. "You're a street-dog! Get out, you street-dog!" they yells. And as they drives me out, the pipe-clay drops off me, and they laugh and shriek; and when I looks down I see that I have turned into a black-and-tan.

They was most awful dreams, and next morning, when Miss Dorothy comes and gives me water in a pan, I begs and begs her to take me home, but she can't understand. "How well Kid is!" she says. And when I jumps into the the Master's arms, and pulls to break my chain, he says, "If he knew all as he had against him, miss, he wouldn't be so gay." And from a book they reads out the names of the beautiful high-bred terriers which I have got to meet. And I can't make 'em understand that I only want to run away, and hide myself where no one will see me.

Then suddenly men comes hurrying down our street and begins to brush the beautiful bull-terriers, and Nolan rubs me with a towel so excited that his hands trembles awful, and Miss Dorothy tweaks my ears between her gloves, so that the blood runs to 'em, and they turn pink and stand straight and sharp.

"Now, then, Nolan," says she, her voice shaking just like his fingers, "keep his head up—and never let the Judge lose sight of him." When I hears that my legs breaks under me, for I knows all about judges. Twice, the old Master goes up before the Judge for fighting me with other dogs, and the Judge promises him if he ever does it again, he'll chain him up in jail. I knew he'd find me out. A Judge can't be fooled by no pipe-clay. He can see right through you, and he reads your insides.

The judging-ring, which is where the Judge holds out, was so like a fighting-pit, that when I came in it, and find six other dogs there, I springs into position, so that when they lets us go I can defend myself. But the Master smoothes down my hair and whispers, "Hold 'ard, Kid, hold 'ard. This ain't a fight," says he. "Look your prettiest," he whispers. "Please, Kid, look your prettiest," and he pulls my leash so tight that I can't touch my pats to the sawdust, and my nose goes up in the air. There was millions of people a-watching us from the railings, and three of our kennel-men, too, making fun of Nolan and me, and Miss Dorothy with her chin just reaching to the rail, and her eyes so big that I thought she was a-going to cry. It was awful to think that when the Judge stood up and exposed me, all those people, and Miss Dorothy, would be there to see me driven from the show.

The Judge, he was a fierce-looking man with specs on his nose, and a red beard. When I first come in he didn't see me owing to my being too quick for him and dodging behind the Master. But when the Master drags me round and I pulls at the sawdust to keep back, the Judge looks at us careless-like, and then stops and glares through his specs, and I knew it was all up with me.

"Are there any more?" asks the Judge, to the gentleman at the gate, but never taking his specs from me.

The man at the gate looks in his book. "Seven in the novice-class," says he. "They're all here. You can go ahead," and he shuts the gate.

The Judge, he doesn't hesitate a moment. He just waves his hand toward the corner of the ring. "Take him away," he says to the Master. "Over there and keep him away," and he turns and looks most solemn at the six beautiful bull-terriers. I don't know how I crawled to that corner. I wanted to scratch under the sawdust and dig myself a grave. The kennel-men they slapped the rail with their hands and laughed at the Master like they would fall over. They pointed at me in the corner, and their sides just shaked. But little Miss Dorothy she presses her lips tight against the rail, and I see tears rolling from her eyes. The Master, he hangs his head like he had been whipped. I felt most sorry for him, than all. He was so red, and he was letting on not to see the kennel-men, and blinking his eyes. If the Judge had ordered me right out, it wouldn't have disgraced us so, but it was keeping me there while he was judging the high-bred dogs that hurt so hard. With all those people staring too. And his doing it so quick, without no doubt nor questions. You can't fool the judges. They see insides you.

But he couldn't make up his mind about them high-bred dogs. He scowls at 'em, and he glares at 'em, first with his head on the one side and then on the other. And he feels of 'em, and orders 'em to run about. And Nolan leans against the rails, with his head hung down, and pats me. And Miss Dorothy comes over beside him, but don't say nothing, only wipes her eye with her finger. A man on the other side of the rail he says to the Master, "The Judge don't like your dog?"

"No," says the Master.

"Have you ever shown him before?" says the man.

"No," says the Master, "and I'll never show

him again. He's my dog," says the Master,
"an' he suits me! And I don't care what no
judges think." And when he says them kind
words, I licks his hand most grateful.

The Judge had two of the six dogs on a little
platform in the middle of the ring, and he
had chased the four other dogs into the cor-
ners, where they was licking their chops, and
letting on they didn't care, same as Nolan
was.

The two dogs on the platform was so beautiful
that the Judge hisself couldn't tell which was
the best of 'em, even when he stoops down and
holds their heads together. But at last he gives
a sigh, and brushes the sawdust off his knees
and goes to the table in the ring, where there
was a man keeping score, and heaps and heaps
of blue and gold and red and yellow ribbons.
And the Judge picks up a bunch of 'em and
walks to the two gentlemen who was holding
the beautiful dogs, and he says to each "What's
his number?" and he hands each gentleman a
ribbon. And then he turned sharp, and comes
straight at the Master.

"What's his number?" says the Judge. And
Master was so scared that he couldn't make no
answer.

But Miss Dorothy claps her hands and cries
out like she was laughing, "Three twenty-six,"

and the Judge writes it down, and shoves Master the blue ribbon.

I bit the Master, and I jumps and bit Miss Dorothy, and I waggled so hard that the Master couldn't hold me. When I get to the gate Miss Dorothy snatches me up and kisses me between the ears, right before millions of people, and they both hold me so tight that I didn't know which of them was carrying of me. But one thing I knew, for I listened hard, as it was the Judge hisself as said it.

"Did you see that puppy I gave 'first' to?" says the judge to the gentleman at the gate.

"I did. He was a bit out of his class," says the gate-gentleman.

"He certainly was!" says the Judge, and they both laughed.

But I didn't care. They couldn't hurt me then, not with Nolan holding the blue ribbon and Miss Dorothy hugging my ears, and the kennel-men sneaking away, each looking like he'd been caught with his nose under the lid of the slop-can.

We sat down together, and we all three just talked as fast as we could. They was so pleased that I couldn't help feeling proud myself, and barked and jumped and leaped about so gay, that all the bull-terriers in our street stretched on their chains, and howled at me.

"Just look at him!" says one of those I had beat. "What's he giving hisself airs about?"

"Because he's got one blue ribbon!" says another of 'em. "Why, when I was a puppy I used to eat 'em, and if that Judge could ever learn to know a toy from a mastiff, I'd have had this one."

But Jimmy Jocks he leaned over from his bench, and says, "Well done, Kid. Didn't I tell you so!" What he 'ad told me was that I might get a "commended," but I didn't remind him.

"Didn't I tell you," says Jimmy Jocks, "that I saw your grandfather make his début at the Crystal——"

"Yes, sir, you did, sir," says I, for I have no love for the men of my family.

A gentleman with a showing leash around his neck comes up just then and looks at me very critical. "Nice dog you've got, Miss Wyndham," says he; "would you care to sell him?"

"He's not my dog," says Miss Dorothy, holding me tight. "I wish he were."

"He's not for sale, sir," says the Master, and I was *that* glad.

"Oh, he's yours, is he?" says the gentleman, looking hard at Nolan. "Well, I'll give you a hundred dollars for him," says he, careless-like.

"Thank you, sir, he's not for sale," says Nolan,

out his eyes get very big. The gentleman, he walked away, but I watches him, and he talks to a man in a golf-cap, and by and by the man comes along our street, looking at all the dogs, and stops in front of me.

"This your dog?" says he to Nolan. "Pity he's so leggy," says he. "If he had a good tail, and a longer stop, and his ears were set higher, he'd be a good dog. As he is, I'll give you fifty dollars for him."

But, before the Master could speak, Miss Dorothy laughs, and says, "You're Mr. Polk's kennel-man, I believe. Well, you tell Mr. Polk from me that the dog's not for sale now any more than he was five minutes ago, and that when he is, he'll have to bid against me for him." The man looks foolish at that, but he turns to Nolan quick-like. "I'll give you three hundred for him," he says.

"Oh, indeed!" whispers Miss Dorothy, like she was talking to herself. "That's it, is it," and she turns and looks at me as though she had never seen me before. Nolan, he was gaping, too, with his mouth open. But he holds me tight.

"He's not for sale," he growls, like he was frightened, and the man looks black and walks away.

"Why, Nolan!" cries Miss Dorothy, "Mr.

Polk knows more about bull-terriers than any amateur in America. What can he mean? Why, Kid is no more than a puppy! Three hundred dollars for a puppy!"

"And he ain't no thoroughbred neither!" cries the Master. "He's 'Unknown,' ain't he? Kid can't help it, of course, but his mother, Miss——"

I dropped my head. I couldn't bear he should tell Miss Dorothy. I couldn't bear she should know I had stolen my blue ribbon.

But the Master never told, for at that, a gentleman runs up, calling, "Three Twenty-Six, Three Twenty-Six," and Miss Dorothy says, "Here he is, what is it?"

"The Winner's Class," says the gentleman. "Hurry, please. The Judge is waiting for him."

Nolan tries to get me off the chain onto a showing leash, but he shakes so, he only chokes me. "What is it, Miss?" he says. "What is it?"

"The Winner's Class," says Miss Dorothy. "The Judge wants him with the winners of the other classes—to decide which is the best. It's only a form," says she. "He has the champions against him now."

"Yes," says the gentleman, as he hurries us to the ring. "I'm afraid it's only a form for your dog, but the Judge wants all the winners, puppy class even."

We had got to the gate, and the gentleman there was writing down my number.

"Who won the open?" asks Miss Dorothy.

"Oh, who would?" laughs the gentleman. "The old champion, of course. He's won for three years now. There he is. Isn't he wonderful?" says he, and he points to a dog that's standing proud and haughty on the platform in the middle of the ring.

I never see so beautiful a dog, so fine and clean and noble, so white like he had rolled hisself in flour, holding his nose up and his eyes shut, same as though no one was worth looking at. Aside of him, we other dogs, even though we had a blue ribbon apiece, seemed like lumps of mud. He was a royal gentleman, a king, he was. His Master didn't have to hold his head with no leash. He held it hisself, standing as still as an iron dog on a lawn, like he knew all the people was looking at him. And so they was, and no one around the ring pointed at no other dog but him.

"Oh, what a picture," cried Miss Dorothy; "he's like a marble figure by a great artist—one who loved dogs. Who is he?" says she, looking in her book. "I don't keep up with terriers."

"Oh, you know him," says the gentleman.

"He is the Champion of champions, Regent Royal."

The Master's face went red.

"And this is Regent Royal's son," cries he, and he pulls me quick into the ring, and plants me on the platform next my father.

I trembled so that I near fall. My legs twisted like a leash. But my father he never looked at me. He only smiled, the same sleepy smile, and he still keep his eyes half-shut, like as no one, no, not even his son, was worth his lookin' at.

The Judge, he didn't let me stay beside my father, but, one by one, he placed the other dogs next to him and measured and felt and pulled at them. And each one he put down, but he never put my father down. And then he comes over and picks up me and sets me back on the platform, shoulder to shoulder with the Champion Regent Royal, and goes down on his knees, and looks into our eyes.

The gentleman with my father, he laughs, and says to the Judge, "Thinking of keeping us here all day, John?" but the Judge, he doesn't hear him, and goes behind us and runs his hand down my side, and holds back my ears, and takes my jaw between his fingers. The crowd around the ring is very deep now, and nobody says nothing. The gentleman at the score-table, he is leaning forward, with his elbows on his knees, and his eyes very wide, and the gentleman at the gate is whispering quick to Miss Dorothy, who has turned white. I stood as stiff as stone. I didn't even breathe. But out of the corner of my eye I could see my father licking his pink chops, and yawning just a little, like he was bored.

The Judge, he had stopped looking fierce, and was looking solemn. Something inside him seemed a troubling him awful. The more he stares at us now, the more solemn he gets, and when he touches us he does it gentle, like he was patting us. For a long time he kneels in the sawdust, looking at my father and at me, and no one around the ring says nothing to nobody.

Then the Judge takes a breath and touches me sudden. "It's his," he says, but he lays his hand just as quick on my father. "I'm sorry," says he.

The gentleman holding my father cries:

"Do you mean to tell me——"

And the Judge, he answers, "I mean the other is the better dog." He takes my father's head between his hands and looks down at him, most sorrowful. "The King is dead," says he, "long live the King. Good-by, Regent," he says.

The crowd around the railings clapped their

hands, and some laughed scornful, and every one talks fast, and I start for the gate so dizzy that I can't see my way. But my father pushes in front of me, walking very daintily, and smiling sleepy, same as he had just been waked, with his head high, and his eyes shut, looking at nobody.

So that is how I "came by my inheritance," as Miss Dorothy calls it, and just for that, though I couldn't feel where I was any different, the crowd follows me to my bench, and pats me, and coos at me, like I was a baby in a baby-carriage. And the handlers have to hold 'em back so that the gentlemen from the papers can make pictures of me, and Nolan walks me up and down so proud, and the men shakes their heads and says, "He certainly is the true type, he is!" And the pretty ladies asks Miss Dorothy, who sits beside me letting me lick her gloves to show the crowd what friends we is, "Aren't you afraid he'll bite you?" and Jimmy Jocks calls to me, "Didn't I tell you so! I always knew you were one of us. Blood will out, Kid, blood will out. I saw your grandfather," says he, "make his début at the Crystal Palace. But he was never the dog you are!"

After that, if I could have asked for it, there was nothing I couldn't get. You might have thought I was a snow-dog, and they was afeerd

I'd melt. If I wet my pats, Nolan gave me a hot bath and chained me to the stove; if I couldn't eat my food, being stuffed full by the cook, for I am a house-dog now, and let in to lunch whether there is visitors or not, Nolan would run to bring the vet. It was all tommy-rot, as Jimmy says, but meant most kind. I couldn't scratch myself comfortable, without Nolan giving me nasty drinks, and rubbing me outside till it burnt awful, and I wasn't let to eat bones for fear of spoiling my "beautiful" mouth, what mother used to call my "punishing jaw," and my food was cooked special on a gas-stove, and Miss Dorothy gives me an overcoat, cut very stylish like the champions', to wear when we goes out carriage-driving.

After the next show, where I takes three blue ribbons, four silver cups, two medals, and brings home forty-five dollars for Nolan, they gives me a "Registered" name, same as Jimmy's. Miss Dorothy wanted to call me "Regent Heir Apparent," but I was THAT glad when Nolan says, "No, Kid don't owe nothing to his father, only to you and hisself. So, if you please, Miss, we'll call him Wyndham Kid." And so they did, and you can see it on my overcoat in blue letters, and painted top of my kennel. It was all too hard to understand. For days I just sat and wondered if I was really me, and

how it all come about, and why everybody was
so kind. But, oh, it was so good they was, for
if they hadn't been, I'd never have got the thing
I most wished after. But, because they was
kind, and not liking to deny me nothing, they
gave it me, and it was more to me than anything
in the world.

It came about one day when we was out driv-
ing. We was in the cart they calls the dog-cart,
because it's the one Miss Dorothy keeps to take
Jimmy and me for an airing. Nolan was up
behind, and me in my new overcoat was sitting
beside Miss Dorothy. I was admiring the view,
and thinking how good it was to have a horse
pull you about so that you needn't get yourself
splashed and have to be washed, when I hears a
dog calling loud for help, and I pricks up my
ears and looks over the horse's head. And I
sees something that makes me tremble down to
my toes. In the road before us three big dogs
was chasing a little, old lady-dog. She had a
string to her tail, where some boys had tied a
can, and she was dirty with mud and ashes,
and torn most awful. She was too far done up
to get away, and too old to help herself, but she
was making a fight for her life, snapping her old
gums savage, and dying game. All this I see
in a wink, and then the three dogs pinned her
down, and I can't stand it no longer and clears

the wheel and lands in the road on my head. It was my stylish overcoat done that, and I curse it proper, but I gets my pats again quick, and makes a rush for the fighting. Behind me I hear Miss Dorothy cry, "They'll kill that old dog. Wait, take my whip. Beat them off her! The Kid can take care of himself," and I hear Nolan fall into the road, and the horse come to a stop. The old lady-dog was down, and the three was eating her vicious, but as I come up, scattering the pebbles, she hears, and thinking it's one more of them, she lifts her head and my heart breaks open like some one had sunk his teeth in it. For, under the ashes and the dirt and the blood, I can see who it is, and I know that my mother has come back to me.

I gives a yell that throws them three dogs off their legs.

"Mother!" I cries. "I'm the Kid," I cries. "I'm coming to you, mother, I'm coming."

And I shoots over her, at the throat of the big dog, and the other two, they sinks their teeth into that stylish overcoat, and tears it off me, and that sets me free, and I lets them have it. I never had so fine a fight as that! What with mother being there to see, and not having been let to mix up in no fights since I become a prize-winner, it just naturally did me good, and it wasn't three shakes before I had 'em yelping.

Quick as a wink, mother, she jumps in to help me, and I just laughed to see her. It was so like old times. And Nolan, he made me laugh too. He was like a hen on a bank, shaking the butt of his whip, but not daring to cut in for fear of hitting me.

"Stop it, Kid," he says, "stop it. Do you want to be all torn up?" says he. "Think of the Boston show next week," says he. "Think of Chicago. Think of Danbury. Don't you never want to be a champion?" How was I to think of all them places when I had three dogs to cut up at the same time. But in a minute two of 'em begs for mercy, and mother and me lets 'em run away. The big one, he ain't able to run away. Then mother and me, we dances and jumps, and barks and laughs, and bites each other and rolls each other in the road. There never was two dogs so happy as we, and Nolan, he whistles and calls and begs me to come to him, but I just laugh and play larks with mother.

"Now, you come with me," says I, "to my new home, and never try to run away again." And I shows her our house with the five red roofs, set on the top of the hill. But mother trembles awful, and says: "They'd never let the likes of me in such a place. Does the Viceroy live there, Kid?" says she. And I laugh at her. "No, I do," I says; "and if they won't let you live there, too, you and me will go back to the streets together, for we must never be parted no more." So we trots up the hill, side by side, with Nolan trying to catch me, and Miss Dorothy laughing at him from the cart.

"The Kid's made friends with the poor old dog," says she. "Maybe he knew her long ago when he ran the streets himself. Put her in here beside me, and see if he doesn't follow."

So, when I hears that, I tells mother to go with Nolan and sit in the cart, but she says no, that she'd soil the pretty lady's frock; but I tells her to do as I say, and so Nolan lifts her, trembling still, into the cart, and I runs alongside, barking joyful.

When we drives into the stables I takes mother to my kennel, and tells her to go inside it and make herself at home. "Oh, but he won't let me!" says she.

"Who won't let you?" says I, keeping my eye on Nolan, and growling a bit nasty, just to show I was meaning to have my way.

"Why, Wyndham Kid," says she, looking up at the name on my kennel.

"But I'm Wyndham Kid!" says I.

"You!" cries mother. "You! Is my little Kid the great Wyndham Kid the dogs all talk about?" And at that, she, being very old, and sick, and hungry, and nervous, as mothers are, just drops down in the straw and weeps bitter.

Well, there ain't much more than that to tell. Miss Dorothy, she settled it.

"If the Kid wants the poor old thing in the stables," says she, "let her stay."

"You see," says she, "she's a black-and-tan, and his mother was a black-and-tan, and maybe that's what makes Kid feel so friendly toward her," says she.

"Indeed, for me," says Nolan, "she can have the best there is. I'd never drive out no dog that asks for a crust nor a shelter," he says. "But what will Mr. Wyndham do?"

"He'll do what I say," says Miss Dorothy, "and if I say she's to stay, she will stay, and I say—she's to stay!"

And so mother and Nolan, and me, found a home. Mother was scared at first—not being used to kind people—but she was so gentle and loving, that the grooms got fonder of her than of me, and tried to make me jealous by patting of her, and giving her the pick of the vittles. But that was the wrong way to hurt my feelings. That's all, I think. Mother is so happy here that I tell her we ought to call it the Happy Hunting Grounds, because no one hunts you, and there is nothing to hunt; it just all comes to you. And so we live in peace, mother sleeping all day in the sun, or behind the stove in the head-groom's office, being fed twice a day regular by Nolan, and all the day by the other grooms most irregular. And, as for me, I go hurrying around the country to the bench-shows; winning money and cups for Nolan, and taking the blue ribbons away from father.

# A QUESTION OF LATITUDE

Of the school of earnest young writers at whom the word muckraker had been thrown in opprobrium, and by whom it had been caught up as a title of honor, Everett was among the younger and less conspicuous. But if in his skirmishes with graft and corruption he had failed to correct the evils he attacked from the contests he himself had always emerged with credit. His sincerity and his methods were above suspicion. No one had caught him in misstatement, or exaggeration. Even those whom he attacked, admitted he fought fair. For these reasons, the editors of magazines with the fear of libel before their eyes, regarded him as a "safe" man, the public, feeling that the evils he exposed were due to its own indifference, with uncomfortable approval, and those he attacked, with impotent anger. Their anger was impotent because, in the case of Everett, the weapons used by their class in "striking back" were denied them. They could not say that for money he sold sensations, because it was known that a proud and wealthy parent supplied him with all the money he wanted

# A QUESTION OF LATITUDE

Nor in his private life could they find anything to offset his attacks upon the misconduct of others. Men had been sent to spy upon him, and women to lay traps. But the men reported that his evenings were spent at his club, and, from the women, those who sent them learned only that Everett "treats a lady just as though she *is* a lady."

Accordingly, when, with much trumpeting, he departed to investigate conditions in the Congo, there were some who rejoiced.

The standard of life to which Everett was accustomed was high. In his home in Boston it had been set for him by a father and mother who, though critics rather than workers in the world, had taught him to despise what was mean and ungenerous, to write the truth and abhor a compromise. At Harvard he had interested himself in municipal reform, and when later he moved to New York, he transferred his interest to the problems of that city. His attack upon Tammany Hall did not utterly destroy that organization, but at once brought him to the notice of the editors. By them he was invited to tilt his lance at evils in other parts of the United States, at "systems," trusts, convict camps, municipal misrule. His work had met with a measure of success that seemed to justify *Lowell's Weekly* in sending

him further afield, and he now was on his way
to tell the truth about the Congo. Personally,
Everett was a healthy, clean-minded enthusiast.
He possessed all of the advantages of youth,
and all of its intolerance. He was supposed to
be engaged to Florence Carey, but he was not.
There was, however, between them an "understanding," which understanding, as Everett
understood it, meant that until she was ready
to say, "I am ready," he was to think of her,
dream of her, write love-letters to her, and
keep himself only for her. He loved her very
dearly, and, having no choice, was content to
wait. His content was fortunate, as Miss
Carey seemed inclined to keep him waiting in-
definitely.

Except in Europe, Everett had never travelled outside the limits of his own country.
But the new land toward which he was advanc-
ing held no terrors. As he understood it, the
Congo was at the mercy of a corrupt "ring."
In every part of the United States he had found
a city in the clutch of a corrupt ring. The conditions would be the same, the methods he
would use to get at the truth would be the
same, the result for reform would be the
same.

The English steamer on which he sailed for
Southampton was one leased by the Indepen-

dent State of the Congo, and, with a few exceptions, her passengers were subjects of King Leopold. On board, the language was French, at table the men sat according to the rank they held in the administration of the jungle, and each in his buttonhole wore the tiny silver star that showed that for three years, to fill the storehouses of the King of the Belgians, he had gathered rubber and ivory. In the smoking-room Everett soon discovered that passengers not in the service of that king, the English and German officers and traders, held aloof from the Belgians. Their attitude toward them seemed to be one partly of contempt, partly of pity.

"Are your English protectorates on the coast, then, so much better administered?" Everett asked.

The English Coaster, who for ten years in Nigeria had escaped fever and sudden death, laughed evasively.

"I have never been in the Congo," he said. "Only know what they tell one. But you'll see for yourself. That is," he added, "you'll see what they want you to see."

They were leaning on the rail, with their eyes turned toward the coast of Liberia, a gloomy green line against which the waves cast up fountains of foam as high as the cocoanut palms. As a subject of discussion, the Coaster seemed anxious to avoid the Congo.

"It was there," he said, pointing, "the *Three Castles* struck on the rocks. She was a total loss. So were her passengers," he added. "They ate them."

Everett gazed suspiciously at the unmoved face of the veteran.

"*Who* ate them?" he asked guardedly. "Sharks?"

"The natives that live back of that shore-line in the lagoons."

Everett laughed with the assurance of one for whom a trap had been laid and who had cleverly avoided it.

"Cannibals," he mocked. "Cannibals went out of date with pirates. But perhaps," he added apologetically, "this happened some years ago?"

"Happened last month," said the trader.

"But Liberia is a perfectly good republic," protested Everett. "The blacks there may not be as far advanced as in your colonies, but they're not cannibals."

"Monrovia is a very small part of Liberia," said the trader dryly. "And none of these protectorates, or crown colonies, on this coast pretends to control much of the Hinterland. There is Sierra Leone, for instance, about the oldest of them. Last year the governor celebrated the hundredth anniversary of the year the British abolished slavery. They had parades and tea-fights, and all the blacks were in the street in straw hats with cricket ribbons, thanking God they were not as other men are, not slaves like their grandfathers. Well, just at the height of the jubilation, the tribes within twenty miles of the town sent in to say that they, also, were holding a palaver, and it was to mark the fact that they *never* had been slaves and never would be, and, if the governor doubted it, to send out his fighting men and they'd prove it. It cast quite a gloom over the celebration."

"Do you mean that only twenty miles from the coast—" began Everett.

"*Ten* miles," said the Coaster. "Wait till you see Calabar. That's our Exhibit A. The cleanest, best administered. Everything there is model: hospitals, barracks, golf links. Last year, ten miles from Calabar, Dr. Stewart rode his bicycle into a native village. The king tortured him six days, cut him up, and sent pieces of him to fifty villages with the message: 'You eat each other. *We* eat white chop.' That was ten miles from our model barracks."

For some moments the muckraker considered the statement thoughtfully.

"You mean," he inquired, "that the atrocities are not all on the side of the white men?"

"Atrocities?" exclaimed the trader. "I wasn't talking of atrocities. Are you looking for them?"

"I'm not running away from them," laughed Everett. "*Lowell's Weekly* is sending me to the Congo to find out the truth, and to try to help put an end to them."

In his turn the trader considered the statement carefully.

"Among the natives," he explained, painstakingly picking each word, "what you call 'atrocities' are customs of warfare, forms of punishment. When they go to war they *expect* to be tortured; they *know*, if they're killed, they'll be eaten. The white man comes here and finds these customs have existed for centuries. He adopts them, because——"

"One moment!" interrupted Everett warmly. "That does not excuse *him*. The point is, that with him they have *not* existed. To him they should be against his conscience, indecent, horrible! He has a greater knowledge, a much higher intelligence; he should lift the native, not sink to him."

The Coaster took his pipe from his mouth, and twice opened his lips to speak. Finally, he blew the smoke into the air, and shook his head.

"What's the use!" he exclaimed.

"Try," laughed Everett. "Maybe I'm not as unintelligent as I talk."

"You must get this right," protested the Coaster. "It doesn't matter a damn what a man *brings* here, what his training *was*, what *he is*. The thing is too strong for him."

"What thing?"

"That!" said the Coaster. He threw out his arm at the brooding mountains, the dark lagoons, the glaring coast-line against which the waves shot into the air with the shock and roar of twelve-inch guns.

"The first white man came to Sierra Leone five hundred years before Christ," said the Coaster. "And, in twenty-two hundred years, he's got just twenty miles inland. The native didn't need forts, or a navy, to stop him. He had three allies: those waves, the fever, and the sun. Especially the sun. The black man goes bare-headed, and the sun lets him pass. The white man covers his head with an inch of cork, and the sun strikes through it and kills him. When Jameson came down the river from Yam-buya, the natives fired on his boat. He waved his helmet at them for three minutes, to show them there was a white man in the canoe.

63

Three minutes was all the sun wanted. Jameson died in two days. Where you are going, the sun does worse things to a man than kill him: it drives him mad. It keeps the fear of death in his heart; and *that* takes away his nerve and his sense of proportion. He flies into murderous fits, over silly, imaginary slights; he grows morbid, suspicious, he becomes a coward, and because he is a coward with authority, he becomes a bully.

"He is alone, we will suppose, at a station three hundred miles from any other white man. One morning his house-boy spills a cup of coffee on him, and in a rage he half kills the boy. He broods over that, until he discovers, or his crazy mind makes him think he has discovered, that in revenge the boy is plotting to poison him. So he punishes him again. Only this time he punishes him as the black man has taught him to punish, in the only way the black man seems to understand; that is, he tortures him. From that moment the fall of that man is rapid. The heat, the loneliness, the fever, the fear of the black faces, keep him on edge, rob him of sleep, rob him of his physical strength, of his moral strength. He loses shame, loses reason; becomes cruel, weak, degenerate. He invents new, bestial tortures; commits new, unspeakable 'atrocities,' until, one day, the natives turn and kill him, or he

sticks his gun in his mouth and blows the top
of his head off."

The Coaster smiled tolerantly at the wide-
eyed, eager young man at his side.

"And you," he mocked, "think you can reform that man, and that hell above ground
called the Congo, with an article in *Lowell's
Weekly?*"

Undismayed, Everett grinned cheerfully.

"That's what I'm here for!" he said.

By the time Everett reached the mouth of
the Congo, he had learned that in everything
he must depend upon himself; that he would
be accepted only as the kind of man that, at
the moment, he showed himself to be. This
attitude of independence was not chosen, but
forced on him by the men with whom he came
in contact. Associations and traditions, that
in every part of the United States had served
as letters of introduction, and enabled strangers
to identify and label him, were to the white
men on the steamer and at the ports of call
without meaning or value. That he was an
Everett of Boston conveyed little to those who
had not heard even of Boston. That he was
the correspondent of *Lowell's Weekly* meant less
to those who did not know that *Lowell's Weekly*
existed. And when, in confusion, he proffered
his letter of credit, the very fact that it called
for a thousand pounds was, in the eyes of a

"Palm Oil Ruffian," sufficient evidence that it had been forged or stolen. He soon saw that solely as a white man was he accepted and made welcome. That he was respectable, few believed, and no one cared. To be taken at his face value, to be refused at the start the benefit of the doubt, was a novel sensation; and yet not unpleasant. It was a relief not to be accepted only as Everett the Muckraker, as a professional reformer, as one holier than others. It afforded his soul the same relaxation that his body received when, in his shirt-sleeves in the sweltering smoking-room, he drank beer with a *chef de poste* who had been thrice tried for murder.

Not only to every one was he a stranger, but to him everything was strange; so strange as to appear unreal. This did not prevent him from at once recognizing those things that were not strange, such as corrupt officials, incompetence, mismanagement. He did not need the missionaries to point out to him that the Independent State of the Congo was not a colony administered for the benefit of many, but a vast rubber plantation worked by slaves to fill the pockets of one man. It was not in his work that Everett found himself confused. It was in his attitude of mind toward almost every other question.

# A QUESTION OF LATITUDE

At first, when he could not make everything fit his rule of thumb, he excused the country tolerantly as a "topsy-turvy" land.  He wished to move and act quickly; to make others move quickly.  He did not understand that men who had sentenced themselves to exile for the official term of three years, or for life, measured time only by the date of their release.  When he learned that even a cablegram could not reach his home in less than eighteen days, that the missionaries to whom he brought letters were a three-months' journey from the coast and from each other, his impatience was chastened to wonder, and, later, to awe.

His education began at Matadi, where he waited until the river steamer was ready to start for Leopoldville.  Of the two places he was assured Matadi was the better, for the reason that if you still were in favor with the steward of the ship that brought you south, he might sell you a piece of ice.

Matadi was a great rock, blazing with heat.  Its narrow, perpendicular paths seemed to run with burning lava.  Its top, the main square of the settlement, was of baked clay, beaten hard by thousands of naked feet.  Crossing it by day was an adventure.  The air that swept it was the breath of a blast-furnace.

Everett found a room over the shop of a

Portuguese trader. It was caked with dirt, and smelled of unnamed diseases and chloride of lime. In it was a canvas cot, a roll of evil-looking bedding, a wash-basin filled with the stumps of cigarettes. In a corner was a tin chop-box, which Everett asked to have removed. It belonged, the landlord told him, to the man who, two nights before, had occupied the cot and who had died in it. Everett was anxious to learn of what he had died. Apparently surprised at the question, the Portuguese shrugged his shoulders.

"Who knows?" he exclaimed. The next morning the English trader across the street assured Everett there was no occasion for alarm. "He didn't die of any disease," he explained. "Somebody got at him from the balcony, while he was in his cot, and knifed him."

The English trader was a young man, a cockney, named Upsher. At home he had been a steward on the Channel steamers. Everett made him his most intimate friend. He had a black wife, who spent most of her day in a four-post bed, hung with lace curtains and blue ribbons, in which she resembled a baby hippopotamus wallowing in a bank of white sand.

At first the black woman was a shock to

68

Everett, but after Upsher dismissed her indifferently as a "good old sort," and spent one evening blubbering over a photograph of his wife and "kiddy" at home, Everett accepted her. His excuse for this was that men who knew they might die on the morrow must not be judged by what they do to-day. The excuse did not ring sound, but he dismissed the doubt by deciding that in such heat it was not possible to take serious questions seriously. In the fact that, to those about him, the thought of death was ever present, he found further excuse for much else that puzzled and shocked him. At home, death had been a contingency so remote that he had put it aside as something he need not consider until he was a grandfather. At Matadi, at every moment of the day, in each trifling act, he found death must be faced, conciliated, conquered. At home he might ask himself, "If I eat this will it give me indigestion?" At Matadi he asked, "If I drink this will I die?"

Upsher told him of a feud then existing between the chief of police and an Italian doctor in the State service. Interested in the outcome only as a sporting proposition, Upsher declared the odds were unfair, because the Belgian was using his black police to act as his body-guard while for protection the Italian could depend only upon his sword-cane. Each night, with the other white exiles of Matadi, the two adversaries met in the Café Franco-Belge. There, with puzzled interest, Everett watched them sitting at separate tables, surrounded by mutual friends, excitedly playing dominoes. Outside the café, Matadi lay smothered and sweltering in a black, living darkness, and, save for the rush of the river, in a silence that continued unbroken across a jungle as wide as Europe. Inside the dominoes clicked, the glasses rang on the iron tables, the oil lamps glared upon the pallid, sweating faces of clerks, upon the tanned, sweating skins of officers; and the Italian doctor and the Belgian lieutenant, each with murder in his heart, laughed, shrugged, gesticulated, waiting for the moment to strike.

"But why doesn't some one *do* something?" demanded Everett. "Arrest them, or reason with them. Everybody knows about it. It seems a pity not to *do* something."

Upsher nodded his head. Dimly he recognized a language with which he once had been familiar. "I know what you mean," he agreed. "Bind 'em over to keep the peace. And a good job, too! But who?" he demanded vaguely. "That's what I say! Who?" From the confusion into which Everett's appeal to forgotten memories had thrown it, his mind suddenly emerged. "But what's the use!" he demanded. "Don't you see," he explained triumphantly, "if those two crazy men were fit to listen to *sense*, they'd have sense enough not to kill each other!"

Each succeeding evening Everett watched the two potential murderers with lessening interest. He even made a bet with Upsher, of a bottle of fruit salt, that the chief of police would be the one to die.

A few nights later a man, groaning beneath his balcony, disturbed his slumbers. He cursed the man, and turned his pillow to find the cooler side. But all through the night the groans, though fainter, broke into his dreams. At intervals some traditions of past conduct tugged at Everett's sleeve, and bade him rise and play the good Samaritan. But, indignantly, he repulsed them. Were there not many others' within hearing? Were there not the police? Was it *his* place to bind the wounds of drunken stokers? The groans were probably a trick, to entice him, unarmed, into the night. And so, just before the dawn, when the mists rose, and the groans ceased, Everett, still arguing, sank with a contented sigh into forgetfulness.

When he woke, there was beneath his window much monkey-like chattering, and he looked down into the white face and glazed eyes of the

Italian doctor, lying in the gutter and staring up at him. Below his shoulder-blades a pool of blood shone evilly in the blatant sunlight.

Across the street, on his balcony, Upsher, in pajamas and mosquito boots, was shivering with fever and stifling a yawn. "You lose!" he called.

Later in the day, Everett analyzed his conduct of the night previous. "At home," he told Upsher, "I would have been telephoning for an ambulance, or been out in the street giving the man the 'first-aid' drill. But living as we do here, so close to death, we see things more clearly. Death loses its importance. It's a bromide," he added. "But travel certainly broadens one. Every day I have been in the Congo, I have been assimilating new ideas." Upsher nodded vigorously in assent. An older man could have told Everett that he was assimilating just as much of the Congo as the rabbit assimilates of the boa-constrictor, that first smothers it with saliva and then swallows it.

Everett started up the Congo in a small steamer open on all sides to the sun and rain, and with a paddle-wheel astern that kicked her forward at the rate of four miles an hour. Once every day, the boat tied up to a tree and took on wood to feed her furnace, and Everett talked to the white man in charge of the wood post, or if, as it generally happened, the white man was on his back with fever, dosed him with quinine. On board, except for her captain, and a Finn who acted as engineer, Everett was the only other white man. The black crew and "woodboys" he soon disliked intensely. At first, when Nansen, the Danish captain, and the Finn struck them, because they were in the way, or because they were not, Everett winced, and made a note of it. But later he decided the blacks were insolent, sullen, ungrateful; that a blow did them no harm.

According to the unprejudiced testimony of those who, before the war, in his own country, had owned slaves, those of the "Southland" were always content, always happy. When not singing close harmony in the cotton-fields, they danced upon the levee, they twanged the old banjo. But these slaves of the Upper Congo were not happy. They did not dance. They did not sing. At times their eyes, dull, gloomy, despairing, lighted with a sudden sombre fire, and searched the eyes of the white man. They seemed to beg of him the answer to a terrible question. It was always the same question. It had been asked of Pharaoh. They asked it of Leopold. For hours, squatting on the iron deckplates, humped on their naked haunches, crowding close together, they muttered apparently interminable criticisms of Everett. Their eyes never left him. He resented this unceasing scrutiny. It got upon his nerves. He was sure they were evolving some scheme to rob him of his tinned sausages, or, possibly, to kill him. It was then he began to dislike them. In reality, they were discussing the watch strapped to his wrist. They believed it was a powerful juju, to ward off evil spirits. They were afraid of it.

One day, to pay the chief wood-boy for a carved paddle, Everett was measuring a *bras* of cloth. As he had been taught, he held the cloth in his teeth and stretched it to the ends of his finger-tips. The wood-boy thought the white man was giving him short measure. White men always *had* given him short measure, and, at a glance, he could not recognize that this one was an Everett of Boston.

So he opened Everett's fingers.

All the blood in Everett's body leaped to his head. That he, a white man, an Everett, who had come so far to set these people free, should be accused by one of them of petty theft!

He caught up a log of fire wood and laid open the scalp of the black boy, from the eye to the crown of his head. The boy dropped, and Everett, seeing the blood creeping through his kinky wool, turned ill with nausea. Drunkenly, through a red cloud of mist, he heard himself shouting, "The *black* nigger! The *black* nigger! He touched me! I *tell* you, he touched me!" Captain Nansen led Everett to his cot and gave him fizzy salts, but it was not until sundown that the trembling and nausea ceased.

Then, partly in shame, partly as a bribe, he sought out the injured boy and gave him the entire roll of cloth. It had cost Everett ten francs. To the wood-boy it meant a year's wages. The boy hugged it in his arms, as he might a baby, and crooned over it. From under the blood-stained bandage, humbly, without resentment, he lifted his tired eyes to those of the white man. Still, dumbly, they begged the answer to the same question.

During the five months Everett spent up the river he stopped at many missions, stations, one-man wood posts. He talked to Jesuit fathers, to *inspecteurs*, to collectors for the State of rubber, taxes, elephant tusks, in time, even in Bengalese, to chiefs of the native villages. According to the point of view, he was told tales of oppression, of avarice, of hideous crimes, of cruelties committed in the name of trade that were abnormal, unthinkable. The note never was of hope, never of cheer, never inspiring. There was always the grievance, the spirit of unrest, of rebellion that ranged from dislike to a primitive, hot hate. Of his own land and life he heard nothing, not even when his face was again turned toward the east. Nor did he think of it. As now he saw them, the rules and principles and standards of his former existence were petty and credulous. But he assured himself he had not abandoned those standards. He had only temporarily laid them aside, as he had left behind him in London his frock-coat and silk hat. Not because he would not use them again, but because in the Congo they were ridiculous.

For weeks, with a missionary as a guide, he walked through forests into which the sun never penetrated, or, on the river, moved between banks where no white man had placed his foot; where, at night, the elephants came trooping to the water, and, seeing the lights of the boat, fled crashing through the jungle; where the great hippos, puffing and blowing, rose so close to his elbow that he could have tossed his cigarette and hit them. The vastness of the Congo, toward which he had so jauntily set forth, now weighed upon his soul. The immeasurable distances; the slumbering disregard of time; the brooding, interminable silences; the efforts to conquer the land that were so futile, so puny, and so cruel, at first appalled and, later, left him unnerved, rebellious, childishly defiant.

# A QUESTION OF LATITUDE

What health was there, he demanded hotly, in holding in a dripping jungle to morals, to etiquette, to fashions of conduct? Was he, the white man, intelligent, trained, disciplined in mind and body, to be judged by naked cannibals, by chattering monkeys, by mammoth primeval beasts? His code of conduct was his own. He was a law unto himself.

He came down the river on one of the larger steamers of the State, and, on this voyage, with many fellow-passengers. He was now on his way home, but in the fact he felt no elation. Each day the fever ran tingling through his veins, and left him listless, frightened, or choleric. One night at dinner, in one of these moods of irritation, he took offense at the act of a lieutenant who, in lack of vegetables, drank from the vinegar bottle. Everett protested that such table manners were unbecoming an officer, even an officer of the Congo; and on the lieutenant resenting his criticism, Everett drew his revolver. The others at the table took it from him, and locked him in his cabin. In the morning, when he tried to recall what had occurred, he could remember only that, for some excellent reason, he had hated some one with a hatred that could be served only with death. He knew it could not have been drink, as each day the State allowed him but one half-bottle of claret. That but for the interference of strangers he might have shot a man, did not interest him. In the outcome of what he regarded merely as an incident, he saw cause neither for congratulation or self-reproach. For his conduct he laid the blame upon the sun, and doubled his dose of fruit salts.

Everett was again at Matadi, waiting for the *Nigeria* to take on cargo before returning to Liverpool. During the few days that must intervene before she sailed, he lived on board. Although now actually bound north, the thought afforded him no satisfaction. His spirits were depressed, his mind gloomy; a feeling of rebellion, of outlawry, filled him with unrest.

While the ship lay at the wharf, Hardy, her English captain, Cuthbert, the purser, and Everett ate on deck under the awning, assailed by electric fans. Each was clad in nothing more intricate than pajamas.

"To-night," announced Hardy, with a sigh, "we got to dress ship. Mr. Ducret and his wife are coming on board. We carry his trade goods, and I got to stand him a dinner and champagne. You boys," he commanded, "must wear 'whites,' and talk French."

"I'll dine on shore," growled Everett.

"Better meet them," advised Cuthbert. The **purser** was a pink-cheeked, clear-eyed young man, who spoke the many languages of the coast glibly, and his own in the soft, detached voice of a well-bred Englishman. He was in training to enter the consular service. Something in his poise, in the assured manner in which he handled his white stewards and the black Kroo boys, seemed to Everett a constant reproach, and he resented him.

"They're a picturesque couple," explained Cuthbert. "Ducret was originally a wrestler. Used to challenge all comers from the front of a booth. He served his time in the army in Senegal, and when he was mustered out moved to the French Congo and began to trade, in a small way, in ivory. Now he's the biggest merchant, physically and every other way, from Stanley Pool to Lake Chad. He has a house at Brazzaville built of mahogany, and a grand piano, and his own ice-plant. His wife was a supper-girl at Maxim's. He brought her down here and married her. Every rainy season they go back to Paris and run race-horses, and they say the best table in every all-night restaurant is reserved for him. In Paris they call her the Ivory Queen. She's killed seventeen elephants with her own rifle."

In the Upper Congo, Everett had seen four white women. They were pallid, washed-out, bloodless; even the youngest looked past middle-age. For him women of any other type had ceased to exist. He had come to think of every white woman as past middle-age, with a face wrinkled by the sun, with hair bleached white by the sun, with eyes from which, through gazing at the sun, all light and lustre had departed. He thought of them as always wearing boots to protect their ankles from mosquitoes, and army helmets.

When he came on deck for dinner, he saw a woman who looked as though she was posing for a photograph by Reutlinger. She appeared to have stepped to the deck directly from her electric victoria, and the Rue de la Paix. She was tall, lithe, gracefully erect, with eyes of great loveliness, and her hair brilliantly black, drawn, à la Merode, across a broad, fair forehead. She wore a gown and long coat of white lace, as delicate as a bridal veil, and a hat with a flapping brim from which, in a curtain, hung more lace. When she was pleased, she lifted her head and the curtain rose, unmasking her lovely eyes. Around the white, bare throat was a string of pearls. They had cost the lives of many elephants.

Cuthbert, only a month from home, saw Madame Ducret just as she was—a Parisienne, elegant, smart, soigné. He knew that on any night at Madrid or d'Armenonville he might look upon twenty women of the same charming type. They might lack that something this girl from Maxim's possessed—the spirit that had caused her to follow her husband into the depths of darkness. But outwardly, for show purposes, they were even as she.

But to Everett she was no messenger from another world. She was unique. To his famished eyes, starved senses, and fever-driven brain, she was her entire sex personified. She was the one woman for whom he had always sought, alluring, soothing, maddening; if need be, to be fought for; the one thing to be desired. Opposite, across the table, her husband, the ex-wrestler, *chasseur d'Afrique*, elephant poacher, bulked large as an ox. Men felt as well as saw his bigness. Captain Hardy deferred to him on matters of trade. The purser deferred to him on questions of administration. He answered them in his big way, with big thoughts, in big figures. He was fifty years ahead of his time. He beheld the Congo open to the world; in the forests where he had hunted elephants he foresaw great "factories," mining camps, railroads, feeding gold and copper ore to the trunk line, from the Cape to Cairo. His ideas were the ideas of an empire-builder. But, while the others listened, fascinated, hypnotized, Everett saw only the woman, her eyes fixed on her husband, her fingers turning and twisting her diamond rings. Every now and again she raised her eyes to Everett almost reproachfully, as though to say, "Why do you not listen to him? It is much better for you than to look at me."

When they had gone, all through the sultry night, until the sun drove him to his cabin, like a caged animal Everett paced and repaced the deck. The woman possessed his mind and he could not drive her out. He did not wish to drive her out. What the consequences might be he did not care. So long as he might see her again, he jeered at the consequences. Of one thing he was positive. He could not now leave the Congo. He would follow her to Brazzaville. If he were discreet, Ducret might invite him to make himself their guest. Once established in her home, she *must* listen to him. No man ever before had felt for any woman the need he felt for her. It was too big for him to conquer. It would be too big for her to resist.

In the morning a note from Ducret invited Everett and Cuthbert to join him in an all-day excursion to the water-fall beyond Matadi. Everett answered the note in person. The thought of seeing the woman calmed and steadied him like a dose of morphine. So much more violent than the fever in his veins was the fever in his brain that, when again he was with her, he laughed happily, and was grandly at peace. So different was he from the man they had met the night before, that the Frenchman and his wife glanced at each other in surprise and approval. They found him witty, eager, a most charming companion; and when he announced his intention of visiting Brazzaville, they insisted he should make their home his own.

His admiration, as outwardly it appeared to be, for Madame Ducret, was evident to the others, but her husband accepted it. It was her due. And, on the Congo, to grudge to another man the sight of a pretty woman was as cruel as to withhold the few grains of quinine that might save his reason. But before the day passed, Madame Ducret was aware that the American could not be lightly dismissed as an admirer. The fact neither flattered nor offended. For her it was no novel or disturbing experience. Other men, whipped on by loneliness, by fever, by primitive savage instincts, had told her what she meant to them. She did not hold them responsible. Some, worth curing, she had nursed through the illness. Others, who refused to be cured, she had turned over, with a shrug, to her husband. This one was more difficult. Of men of Everett's traditions and education she had known but few; but she recognized the type. This young man was no failure in life, no derelict, no outcast flying the law, or a scandal, to hide in the jungle. He was what, in her Maxim days, she had laughed at as an aristocrat. He knew her Paris as she did not know it: its history, its art. Even her language he spoke more correctly than her husband or herself. She knew that at his home there must be many women infinitely more attractive, more suited to him, than herself: women of birth, of position; young girls and great ladies of the other world. And she knew, also, that, in his present state, at a nod from her he would cast these behind him and carry her into the wilderness. More quickly than she anticipated, Everett proved she did not overrate the forces that compelled him.

The excursion to the rapids was followed by a second dinner on board the *Nigeria*. But now, as on the previous night, Everett fell into sullen silence. He ate nothing, drank continually, and with his eyes devoured the woman. When coffee had been served, he left the others at table, and with Madame Ducret slowly paced the deck. As they passed out of the reach of the lights, he drew her to the rail, and stood in front of her.

"I am not quite mad," he said, "but you have got to come with me."

To Everett all he added to this sounded sane and final. He told her that this was one of those miracles when the one woman and the one man who were predestined to meet had met. He told her he had wished to marry a girl at home, but that he now saw that the desire was the fancy of a school-boy. He told her he was rich, and offered her the choice of returning to the Paris she loved, or of going deeper into the jungle. There he would set up for her a principality, a state within the State. He would defend her against all comers. He would make her the Queen of the Congo.

"I have waited for you thousands of years!" he told her. His voice was hoarse, shaken, and thick. "I love you as men loved women in the Stone Age—fiercely, entirely. I will not be denied. Down here we are cave people, if you fight me, I will club you and drag you to my cave. If others fight for you, I will *kill* them. I love you," he panted, "with all my soul, my mind, my body, I love you! I will not let you go!"

Madame Ducret did not say she was insulted, because she did not feel insulted. She did not call to her husband for help, because she did not need his help, and because she knew that the ex-wrestler could break Everett across his knee. She did not even withdraw her hands, although Everett drove the diamonds deep into her fingers.

"You frighten me!" she pleaded. She was not in the least frightened. She only was sorry that this one must be discarded among the incurables.

In apparent agitation, she whispered, "To-morrow! To-morrow I will give you your answer."

Everett did not trust her, did not release her. He regarded her jealously, with quick suspicion. To warn her that he knew she could not escape from Matadi, or from him, he said, "The train to Leopoldville does not leave for two days!"

"I know!" whispered Madame Ducret soothingly. "I will give you your answer to-morrow at ten." She emphasized the hour, because she knew at sunrise a special train would carry her husband and herself to Leopoldville, and that there one of her husband's steamers would bear them across the Pool to French Congo.

"To-morrow, then!" whispered Everett, grudgingly. "But I must kiss you now!"

Only an instant did Madame Ducret hesitate. Then she turned her cheek. "Yes," she assented. "You must kiss me now."

Everett did not rejoin the others. He led her back into the circle of light, and locked himself in his cabin.

# A QUESTION OF LATITUDE

At ten the next morning, when Ducret and his wife were well advanced toward Stanley Pool, Cuthbert handed Everett a note. Having been told what it contained, he did not move away, but, with his back turned, leaned upon the rail.

Everett, his eyes on fire with triumph, his fingers trembling, tore open the envelope.

Madame Ducret wrote that her husband and herself felt that Mr. Everett was suffering more severely from the climate than he knew. With regret they cancelled their invitation to visit them, and urged him, for his health's sake, to continue as he had planned, to northern latitudes. They hoped to meet in Paris. They extended assurances of their distinguished consideration.

Slowly, savagely, as though wreaking his suffering on some human thing, Everett tore the note into minute fragments. Moving unsteadily to the ship's side, he flung them into the river, and then hung limply upon the rail.

Above him, from a sky of brass, the sun stabbed at his eyeballs. Below him, the rush of the Congo, churning in muddy whirlpools, echoed against the hills of naked rock that met the naked sky.

To Everett, the roar of the great river, and the echoes from the land he had set out to reform, carried the sound of gigantic, hideous laughter.

# THE SPY

My going to Valencia was entirely an accident. But the more often I stated that fact, the more satisfied was every one at the capital that I had come on some secret mission. Even the venerable politician who acted as our minister, the night of my arrival, after dinner, said confidentially, "Now, Mr. Crosby, between ourselves, what's the game?"

"What's what game?" I asked.

"You know what I mean," he returned. "What are you here for?"

But when, for the tenth time, I repeated how I came to be marooned in Valencia he showed that his feelings were hurt, and said stiffly: "As you please. Suppose we join the ladies."

And the next day his wife reproached me with: "I should think you could trust your own minister. My husband *never* talks—not even to me."

"So I see," I said.

And then her feelings were hurt also, and she went about telling people I was an agent of the Walker-Keefe crowd.

My only reason for repeating here that my

going to Valencia was an accident is that it was
because Schnitzel disbelieved that fact, and to
drag the hideous facts from me followed me
back to New York. Through that circumstance
I came to know him, and am able to tell this
story.

The simple truth was that I had been sent by
the State Department to Panama, to "go, look,
see," and straighten out a certain conflict of
authority among the officials of the canal zone.
While I was there the yellow-fever broke out,
and every self-respecting power clapped a quar-
antine on the Isthmus, with the result that
when I tried to return to New York no steamer
would take me to any place to which any white
man would care to go. But I knew that at
Valencia there was a direct line to New York,
so I took a tramp steamer down the coast to
Valencia. I went to Valencia only because to
me every other port in the world was closed.
My position was that of the man who explained
to his wife that he came home because the
other places were shut.

But, because, formerly in Valencia I had held
a minor post in our legation, and because the
State Department so constantly consults our
firm on questions of international law, it was
believed I revisited Valencia on some mysterious
and secret mission.

As a matter of fact, had I gone there to sell phonographs or to start a steam laundry, I should have been as greatly suspected. For in Valencia even every commercial salesman, from the moment he gives up his passport on the steamer until the police permit him to depart, is suspected, shadowed, and begirt with spies.

I believe that during my brief visit I enjoyed the distinction of occupying the undivided attention of three: a common or garden Government spy, from whom no guilty man escapes, a Walker-Keefe spy, and the spy of the Nitrate Company. The spy of the Nitrate Company is generally a man you meet at the legations and clubs. He plays bridge and is dignified with the title of "agent." The Walker-Keefe spy is ostensibly a travelling salesman or hotel runner. The Government spy is just a spy—a scowling, important little beast in a white duck suit and a diamond ring. The limit of his intelligence is to follow you into a cigar store and note what cigar you buy, and in what kind of money you pay for it.

The reason for it all was the three-cornered fight which then was being waged by the Government, the Nitrate Trust, and the Walker-Keefe crowd for the possession of the nitrate beds. Valencia is so near to the equator, and so far from New York, that there are few who studied the intricate story of that disgraceful struggle, which, I hasten to add, with the fear of libel before my eyes, I do not intend to tell now.

Briefly, it was a triangular fight between opponents each of whom was in the wrong, and each of whom, to gain his end, bribed, blackmailed, and robbed, not only his adversaries, but those of his own side, the end in view being the possession of those great deposits that lie in the rocks of Valencia, baked from above by the tropic sun and from below by volcanic fires. As one of their engineers, one night in the Plaza, said to me: "Those mines were conceived in hell, and stink to heaven, and the reputation of every man of us that has touched them smells like the mines."

At the time I was there the situation was "acute." In Valencia the situation always is acute, but this time it looked as though something might happen. On the day before I departed the Nitrate Trust had cabled vehemently for war-ships, the Minister of Foreign Affairs had refused to receive our minister, and at Porto Banos a mob had made the tin sign of the United States consulate look like a sieve. Our minister urged me to remain. To be bombarded by one's own war-ships, he assured me, would be a thrilling experience.

But I repeated that my business was with

Panama, not Valencia, and that if in this matter of his row I had any weight at Washington, as between preserving the nitrate beds for the trust, and preserving for his country and various sweethearts one brown-throated, clean-limbed bluejacket, I was for the bluejacket.

Accordingly, when I sailed from Valencia the aged diplomat would have described our relations as strained.

Our ship was a slow ship, listed to touch at many ports, and as early as noon on the following day we stopped for cargo at Trujillo. It was there I met Schnitzel.

In Panama I had bought a macaw for a little niece of mine, and while we were taking on cargo I went ashore to get a tin cage in which to put it, and, for direction, called upon our consul. From an inner room he entered excitedly, smiling at my card, and asked how he might serve me. I told him I had a parrot below decks, and wanted to buy a tin cage.

"Exactly. You want a tin cage," the consul repeated soothingly. "The State Department doesn't keep me awake nights cabling me what it's going to do," he said, "but at least I know it doesn't send a thousand-dollar-a-minute, four-cylinder lawyer all the way to this fever swamp to buy a tin cage. Now, honest, how can I serve you?" I saw it was hopeless. No one would believe the truth. To offer it to this friendly soul would merely offend his feelings and his intelligence.

So, with much mystery, I asked him to describe the "situation," and he did so with the exactness of one who believes that within an hour every word he speaks will be cabled to the White House.

When I was leaving he said: "Oh, there's a newspaper correspondent after you. He wants an interview, I guess. He followed you last night from the capital by train. You want to watch out he don't catch you. His name is Jones." I promised to be on my guard against a man named Jones, and the consul escorted me to the ship. As he went down the accommodation ladder, I called over the rail: "In case they *should* declare war, cable to Curaçoa, and I'll come back. And don't cable anything indefinite, like 'Situation critical' or 'War imminent.' Understand? Cable me, 'Come back' or 'Go ahead.' But whatever you cable, make it *clear*."

He shook his head violently and with his green-lined umbrella pointed at my elbow. I turned and found a young man hungrily listening to my words. He was leaning on the rail with his chin on his arms and the brim of his Panama hat drawn down to conceal his eyes.

On the pier-head, from which we now were drawing rapidly away, the consul made a megaphone of his hands.

"That's *him*," he called. "That's Jones."

Jones raised his head, and I saw that the tropical heat had made Jones thirsty, or that with friends he had been celebrating his departure. He winked at me, and, apparently with pleasure at his own discernment and with pity for me, smiled.

"Oh, of course!" he murmured. His tone was one of heavy irony. "Make it 'clear.' Make it clear to the whole wharf. Shout it out so's everybody can hear you. You're 'clear' enough." His disgust was too deep for ordinary words. "My uncle!" he exclaimed.

By this I gathered that he was expressing his contempt.

"I beg your pardon?" I said.

We had the deck to ourselves. Its emptiness suddenly reminded me that we had the ship, also, to ourselves. I remembered the purser had told me that, except for those who travelled overnight from port to port, I was his only passenger.

With dismay I pictured myself for ten days adrift on the high seas—alone with Jones.

With a dramatic gesture, as one would say, "I am here!" he pushed back his Panama hat. With an unsteady finger he pointed, as it was drawn dripping across the deck, at the stern hawser.

"You see that rope?" he demanded. "Soon as that rope hit the water I knocked off work. S'long as you was in Valencia—me, on the job. Now, *you* can't go back, *I* can't go back. Why further dissim'lation? *Who am I?*"

His condition seemed to preclude the possibility of his knowing who he was, so I told him.

He sneered as I have seen men sneer only in melodrama.

"Oh, of course," he muttered. "Oh, of course."

He lurched toward me indignantly.

"You know perfec'ly well Jones is not my name. You know perfec'ly well who I am."

"My dear sir," I said, "I don't know anything about you, except that you are a damned nuisance."

He swayed from me, pained and surprised. Apparently he was upon an outbreak of tears.

"Proud," he murmured, "*and* haughty. Proud and haughty to the last."

I never have understood why an intoxicated man feels the climax of insult is to hurl at you your name. Perhaps because he knows it is the one charge you cannot deny. But invariably before you escape, as though assured the words will cover your retreat with shame, he throws at you your full title. Jones did this.

Slowly and mercilessly he repeated, "Mr.—George—Morgan—Crosby. Of Harvard," he added. "Proud and haughty to the last."

He then embraced a passing steward, and demanded to be informed why the ship rolled. He never knew a ship to roll as our ship rolled.

"Perfec'ly satisfact'ry ocean, but ship—rolling like a stone-breaker. Take me some place in the ship where this ship don't roll."

The steward led him away.

When he had dropped the local pilot the captain beckoned me to the bridge.

"I saw you talking to Mr. Schnitzel," he said. "He's a little under the weather. He has too light a head for liquors."

I agreed that he had a light head, and said I understood his name was Jones.

"That's what I wanted to tell you," said the captain. "His name is Schnitzel. He used to work for the Nitrate Trust in New York. Then he came down here as an agent. He's a good boy not to tell things to. Understand? Sometimes I carry him under one name, and the next voyage under another. The purser and he fix it up between 'em. It pleases him, and it don't hurt anybody else, so long as I tell them about it. I don't know who he's working for now," he went on, "but I know he's not with the

Nitrate Company any more. He sold them out."

"How could he?" I asked. "He's only a boy."

"He had a berth as typewriter to Senator Burnsides, president of the Nitrate Trust, sort of confidential stenographer," said the captain. "Whenever the senator dictated an important letter, they say, Schnitzel used to make a carbon copy, and when he had enough of them he sold them to the Walker-Keefe crowd. Then, when Walker-Keefe lost their suit in the Valencia Supreme Court I guess Schnitzel went over to President Alvarez. And again, some folks say he's back with the Nitrate Company."

"After he sold them out?"

"Yes, but you see he's worth more to them now. He knows all the Walker-Keefe secrets and Alvarez's secrets, too."

I expressed my opinion of every one concerned.

"It shouldn't surprise *you*," complained the captain. "You know the country. Every man in it is out for something that isn't his. The pilot wants his bit, the health doctor must get his, the customs take all your cigars, and if you don't put up gold for the captain of the port and the *alcalde* and the commandant and the harbor police and the foreman of the *cargadores*, they won't move a lighter, and they'll hold up the ship's papers. Well, an American comes down here, honest and straight and willing to work for his wages. But pretty quick he finds every one is getting his squeeze but him, so he tries to get some of it back by robbing the natives that robbed him. Then he robs the other foreigners, and it ain't long before he's cheating the people at home who sent him here. There isn't a man in this nitrate row that isn't robbing the crowd he's with, and that wouldn't change sides for money. Schnitzel's no worse than the president nor the canteen contractor."

He waved his hand at the glaring coast-line, at the steaming swamps and the hot, naked mountains.

"It's the country that does it," he said. "It's in the air. You can smell it as soon as you drop anchor, like you smell the slaughter-house at Punta Arenas."

"How do *you* manage to keep honest," I asked, smiling.

"I don't take any chances," exclaimed the captain seriously. "When I'm in their damned port I don't go ashore."

I did not again see Schnitzel until, with haggard eyes and suspiciously wet hair, he joined the captain, doctor, purser, and myself at breakfast. In the phrases of the Tenderloin, he told us cheerfully that he had been grandly intoxicated, and to recover drank mixtures of raw egg, vinegar, and red pepper, the sight of which took away every appetite save his own. When to this he had added a bottle of beer, he declared himself a new man. The new man followed me to the deck, and with the truculent bearing of one who expects to be repelled, he asked if, the day before, he had not made a fool of himself.

I suggested he had been somewhat confidential.

At once he recovered his pose and patronized me.

"Don't you believe it," he said. "That's all part of my game. 'Confidence for confidence' is the way I work it. That's how I learn things. I tell a man something on the inside, and he says: 'Here's a nice young fellow. Nothing stand-offish about him,' and he tells me something he shouldn't. Like as not what I told him wasn't true. See?"

I assured him he interested me greatly.

"You find, then, in your line of business," I asked, "that apparent frankness is advisable? As a rule," I explained, "secrecy is what a—a person in your line—a——"

To save his feelings I hesitated at the word.

"A spy," he said. His face beamed with fatuous complacency.

"But if I had not known you were a spy," I

asked, "would not that have been better for you?"

"In dealing with a party like you, Mr. Crosby," Schnitzel began sententiously, "I use a different method. You're on a secret mission yourself, and you get your information about the nitrate row one way, and I get it another. I deal with you just like we were drummers in the same line of goods. We are rivals in business, but outside of business hours perfect gentlemen."

In the face of the disbelief that had met my denials of any secret mission, I felt to have Schnitzel also disbelieve me would be too great a humiliation. So I remained silent.

"You make your report to the State Department," he explained, "and I make mine to—my people. Who they are doesn't matter. You'd like to know, and I don't want to hurt your feelings, but—that's *my* secret."

My only feelings were a desire to kick Schnitzel heavily, but for Schnitzel to suspect that was impossible. Rather, he pictured me as shaken by his disclosures.

As he hung over the rail the glare of the sun on the tumbling water lit up his foolish, mongrel features, exposed their cunning, their utter lack of any character, and showed behind the shifty eyes the vacant, half-crooked mind.

Schnitzel was smiling to himself with a smile of complete self-satisfaction. In the light of his later conduct, I grew to understand that smile. He had anticipated a rebuff, and he had been received, as he read it, with consideration. The irony of my politeness he had entirely missed. Instead, he read in what I said the admiration of the amateur for the professional. He saw what he believed to be a high agent of the Government treating him as a worthy antagonist. In no other way can I explain his later heaping upon me his confidences. It was the vanity of a child trying to show off.

In ten days, in the limited area of a two-thousand-ton steamer, one could not help but learn something of the history of so communicative a fellow-passenger as Schnitzel. His parents were German and still lived in Germany. But he himself had been brought up on the East Side. An uncle who kept a delicatessen shop in Avenue A had sent him to the public schools and then to a "business college," where he had developed remarkable expertness as' a stenographer. He referred to his skill in this difficult exercise with pitying contempt. Nevertheless, from a room noisy with typewriters this skill had lifted him into the private office of the president of the Nitrate Trust. There, as Schnitzel expressed it, "I saw 'mine,' and I took it." To trace back the criminal instinct that led Schnitzel to steal and sell the private letters of his employer was not difficult. In all of his few early years I found it lying latent. Of every story he told of himself, and he talked only of himself, there was not one that was not to his discredit. He himself never saw this, nor that all he told me showed he was without the moral sense, and with an instinctive enjoyment of what was deceitful, mean, and underhand. That, as I read it, was his character.

In appearance he was smooth-shaven, with long locks that hung behind wide, protruding ears. He had the unhealthy skin of bad blood, and his eyes, as though the daylight hurt them, constantly opened and shut. He was like hundreds of young men that you see loitering on upper Broadway and making predatory raids along the Rialto. Had you passed him in that neighborhood you would have set him down as a wire-tapper, a racing tout, a would-be actor.

As I worked it out, Schnitzel was a spy because it gave him an importance he had not been able to obtain by any other effort. As a child and as a clerk, it was easy to see that among his associates Schnitzel must always have been the butt. Until suddenly, by one dirty action, he had placed himself outside their class. As he expressed it: "Whenever I walk through the office now, where all the stenographers sit, you ought to see those slobs look after me. When they go to the president's door, they got to knock, like I used to, but now, when the old man sees me coming to make my report after one of these trips he calls out, 'Come right in, Mr. Schnitzel.' And like as not I go in with my hat on and offer him a cigar. An' they see me do it, too!"

To me, that speech seemed to give Schnitzel's view of the values of his life. His vanity demanded he be pointed at, if even with contempt. But the contempt never reached him —he only knew that at last people took note of him. They no longer laughed at him, they were afraid of him. In his heart he believed that they regarded him as one who walked in the dark places of world politics, who possessed an evil knowledge of great men as evil as himself, as one who by blackmail held public ministers at his mercy.

This view of himself was the one that he tried to give me. I probably was the first decent man who ever had treated him civilly, and to impress me with his knowledge he spread that knowledge before me. It was *sale*, shocking, degrading.

At first I took comfort in the thought that Schnitzel was a liar. Later, I began to wonder

if all of it were a lie, and finally, in a way I
could not doubt, it was proved to me that the
worst he charged was true.

The night I first began to believe him was
the night we touched at Cristobal, the last port
in Valencia. In the most light-hearted manner
he had been accusing all concerned in the nitrate fight with every crime known in Wal
Street and in the dark reaches of the Congo
River.

"But, I know him, Mr. Schnitzel," I said
sternly. "He is incapable of it. I went to
college with him."

"I don't care whether he's a rah-rah boy or
not," said Schnitzel, "I know that's what he
did when he was up the Orinoco after orchids
and if the tribe had ever caught him they'd
have crucified him. And I know this, too: he
made forty thousand dollars out of the Nitrate
Company on a ten-thousand-dollar job. And
I know it, because he beefed to me about i
himself, because it wasn't big enough."

We were passing the limestone island at the
entrance to the harbor, where, in the prison
fortress, with its muzzle-loading guns pointing
drunkenly at the sky, are buried the politica
prisoners of Valencia.

"Now, there," said Schnitzel, pointing, "tha
shows you what the Nitrate Trust can do

Judge Rojas is in there. He gave the first decision in favor of the Walker-Keefe people, and for making that decision William T. Scott, the Nitrate manager, made Alvarez put Rojas in there. He's seventy years old, and he's been there five years. The cell they keep him in is below the sea-level, and the salt-water leaks through the wall. I've seen it. That's what William T. Scott did, an' up in New York people think 'Billy' Scott is a fine man. I seen him at the Horse Show sitting in a box, bowing to everybody, with his wife sitting beside him, all hung out with pearls. An' that was only a month after I'd seen Rojas in that sewer where Scott put him."

"Schnitzel," I laughed, "you certainly are a magnificent liar."

Schnitzel showed no resentment.

"Go ashore and look for yourself," he muttered. "Don't believe me. Ask Rojas. Ask the first man you meet." He shivered, and shrugged his shoulders. "I tell you, the walls are damp, like sweat."

The Government had telegraphed the commandant to come on board and, as he expressed it, "offer me the hospitality of the port," which meant that I had to take him to the smoking-room and give him champagne. What the Government really wanted was to find out whether I was still on board, and if it were finally rid of me.

I asked the official concerning Judge Rojas.

"Oh, yes," he said readily. "He is still *in-comunicado*."

Without believing it would lead to anything, I suggested:

"It was foolish of him to give offense to Mr. Scott?"

The commandant nodded vivaciously.

"Mr. Scott is very powerful man," he assented. "We all very much love Mr. Scott. The president, he love Mr. Scott, too, but the judges were not sympathetic to Mr. Scott, so Mr. Scott asked our president to give them a warning, and Señor Rojas—he is the warning."

"When will he get out?" I asked.

The commandant held up the glass in the sunlight from the open air-port, and gazed admiringly at the bubbles.

"Who can tell," he said. "Any day when Mr. Scott wishes. Maybe, never. Señor Rojas is an old man. Old, and he has much rheumatics. Maybe, he will never come out to see our beloved country any more."

As we left the harbor we passed so close that one could throw a stone against the wall of the fortress. The sun was just sinking and the air became suddenly chilled. Around the little

sland of limestone the waves swept through the
sea-weed and black manigua up to the rusty
bars of the cells. I saw the barefooted soldiers
smoking upon the sloping ramparts, the common criminals in a long stumbling line bearing
kegs of water, three storm-beaten palms rising
like gallows, and the green and yellow flag of
Valencia crawling down the staff. Somewhere
entombed in that blotched and mildewed ma-
sonry an old man of seventy years was shivering and hugging himself from the damp and
cold. A man who spoke five languages, a just,
brave gentleman. To me it was no new story.
I knew of the horrors of Cristobal prison; of
political rivals chained to criminals loathsome
with disease, of men who had raised the flag of
revolution driven to suicide. But never had I
supposed that my own people could reach from
the city of New York and cast a fellow-man
into that cellar of fever and madness.

As I watched the yellow wall sink into the
sea, I became conscious that Schnitzel was near
me, as before, leaning on the rail, with his chin
sunk on his arms. His face was turned toward
the fortress, and for the first time since I had
known him it was set and serious. And when,
a moment later, he passed me without recognition, I saw that his eyes were filled with fear.

When we touched at Curaçoa I sent a cable

to my sister, announcing the date of my arrival, and then continued on to the Hotel Venezuela. Almost immediately Schnitzel joined me. With easy carelessness he said: "I was in the cable office just now, sending off a wire, and that operator told me he can't make head or tail of the third word in your cable."

"That is strange," I commented, "because it's a French word, and he is French. That's why I wrote it in French."

With the air of one who nails another in a falsehood, Schnitzel exclaimed:

"Then, how did you suppose your sister was going to read it? It's a cipher, that's what it is. Oh, no, *you're* not on a secret mission! Not at all!"

It was most undignified of me, but in five minutes I excused myself, and sent to the State Department the following words:

"Roses red, violets blue, send snow."

Later at the State Department the only person who did not eventually pardon my jest was the clerk who had sat up until three in the morning with my cable, trying to fit it to any known code.

Immediately after my return to the Hotel Venezuela Schnitzel excused himself, and half an hour later returned in triumph with the cable operator and ordered lunch for both. They imbibed much sweet champagne.

When we again were safe at sea, I said:

"Then, how did you suppose your sister was going to read it?"

"Schnitzel, how much did you pay that Frenchman to let you read my second cable?"

Schnitzel's reply was prompt and complacent.

"One hundred dollars gold. It was worth it. Do you want to know how I doped it out?"

I even challenged him to do so. "'Roses red' —war declared; 'violets blue'—outlook bad, or blue; 'send snow'—send squadron, because the white squadron is white like snow. See? It was too easy."

"Schnitzel," I cried, "you are wonderful!"

Schnitzel yawned in my face.

"Oh, you don't have to hit the soles of my feet with a night-stick to keep me awake," he said.

After I had been a week at sea, I found that either I had to believe that in all things Schnitzel was a liar, or that the men of the Nitrate Trust were in all things evil. I was convinced that instead of the people of Valencia robbing them, they were robbing both the people of Valencia and the people of the United States.

To go to war on their account was to degrade our Government. I explained to Schnitzel it was not becoming that the United States navy should be made the cat's-paw of a corrupt corporation. I asked his permission to repeat to the authorities at Washington certain of the statements he had made.

Schnitzel was greatly pleased.

"You're welcome to tell 'em anything I've said," he assented. "And," he added, "most of it's true, too."

I wrote down certain charges he had made, and added what I had always known of the nitrate fight. It was a terrible arraignment. In the evening I read my notes to Schnitzel, who, in a corner of the smoking-room, sat, frowning importantly, checking off each statement, and where I made an error of a date or a name, severely correcting me.

Several times I asked him, "Are you sure this won't get you into trouble with your 'people'? You seem to accuse everybody on each side."

Schnitzel's eyes instantly closed with suspicion.

"Don't you worry about me and my people," he returned sulkily. "That's *my* secret, and you won't find it out, neither. I may be as crooked as the rest of them, but I'm not giving away my employer."

I suppose I looked puzzled.

"I mean not a second time," he added hastily. "I know what you're thinking of, and I got five thousand dollars for it. But now I mean to stick by the men that pay my wages."

"But you've told me enough about each of the three to put any one of them in jail."

"Of course, I have," cried Schnitzel triumphantly.

"If I'd let down on any one crowd you'd know I was working for that crowd, so I've touched 'em all up. Only what I told you about my crowd—isn't true."

The report we finally drew up was so sensational that I was of a mind to throw it overboard. It accused members of the Cabinet, of our Senate, diplomats, business men of national interest, judges of the Valencia courts, private secretaries, clerks, hired bullies, and filibusters. Men the trust could not bribe it had blackmailed. Those it could not corrupt, and they were pitifully few, it crushed with some disgraceful charge.

Looking over my notes, I said:

"You seem to have made every charge except murder."

"How'd I come to leave that out?" Schnitzel answered flippantly. "What about Coleman, the foreman at Bahia, and that German contractor, Ebhardt, and old Smedburg? They talked too much, and they died of yellow-fever, maybe, and maybe what happened to them was they ate knockout drops in their soup."

I disbelieved him, but there came a sudden nasty doubt.

"Curtis, who managed the company's plant

at Barcelona, died of yellow-fever," I said, "and was buried the same day."

For some time Schnitzel glowered uncertainly at the bulkhead.

"Did you know him?" he asked.

"When I was in the legation I knew him well," I said.

"So did I," said Schnitzel. "He wasn't murdered. He murdered himself. He was wrong ten thousand dollars in his accounts. He got worrying about it and we found him outside the clearing with a hole in his head. He left a note saying he couldn't bear the disgrace. As if the company would hold a little grafting against as good a man as Curtis!"

Schnitzel coughed and pretended it was his cigarette.

"You see you don't put in nothing against him," he added savagely.

It was the first time I had seen Schnitzel show emotion, and I was moved to preach.

"Why don't you quit?" I said. "You had an A1 job as a stenographer. Why don't you go back to it?"

"Maybe, some day. But it's great being your own boss. If I was a stenographer, I wouldn't be helping you send in a report to the State Department, would I? No, this job is all right. They send you after something big, and you have the devil of a time getting it, but when you get it, you feel like you had picked a hundred-to-one shot."

The talk or the drink had elated him. His fish-like eyes bulged and shone. He cast a quick look about him. Except for ourselves, the smoking-room was empty. From below came the steady throb of the engines, and from outside the whisper of the waves and of the wind through the cordage. A barefooted sailor pattered by to the bridge. Schnitzel bent toward me, and with his hand pointed to his throat.

"I've got papers on me that's worth a million to a certain party," he whispered. "You understand, my notes in cipher."

He scowled with intense mystery.

"I keep 'em in an oiled-silk bag, tied around my neck with a string. And here," he added hastily, patting his hip, as though to forestall any attack I might make upon his person, "I carry my automatic. It shoots nine bullets in five seconds. They got to be quick to catch me."

"Well, if you have either of those things on you," I said testily, "I don't want to know it. How often have I told you not to talk and drink at the same time?"

"Ah, go on," laughed Schnitzel. "That's an

old gag, warning a fellow not to talk so as to *make* him talk. I do that myself."

That Schnitzel had important papers tied to his neck I no more believe than that he wore a shirt of chain armor, but to please him I pretended to be greatly concerned.

"Now that we're getting into New York," I said, "you must be very careful. A man who carries such important documents on his person might be murdered for them. I think you ought to disguise yourself."

A picture of my bag being carried ashore by Schnitzel in the uniform of a ship's steward rather pleased me.

"Go on, you're kidding!" said Schnitzel. He was drawn between believing I was deeply impressed and with fear that I was mocking him.

"On the contrary," I protested, "I don't feel quite safe myself. Seeing me with you they may think I have papers around *my* neck."

"They wouldn't look at you," Schnitzel reassured me. "They know you're just an amateur. But, as you say, with me, it's different. I *got* to be careful. Now, you mightn't believe it, but I never go near my uncle nor none of my friends that live where I used to hang out. If I did, the other spies would get on my track. I suppose," he went on grandly, "I never go out in New York but that at least two spies are trailing me. But I know how to throw them off. I live 'way downtown in a little hotel you never heard of. You never catch me dining at Sherry's nor the Waldorf. And you never met me out socially, did you, now?"

I confessed I had not.

"And then, I always live under an assumed name."

"Like 'Jones'?" I suggested.

"Well, sometimes 'Jones,'" he admitted.

"To me," I said, "'Jones' lacks imagination. It's the sort of name you give when you're arrested for exceeding the speed limit. Why don't you call yourself Machiavelli?"

"Go on, I'm no dago," said Schnitzel, "and don't you go off thinking 'Jones' is the only disguise I use. But I'm not tellin' what it is, am I? Oh, no."

"Schnitzel," I asked, "have you ever been told that you would make a great detective?"

"Cut it out," said Schnitzel. "You've been reading those fairy stories. There's no fly cops nor Pinks could do the work I do. They're pikers compared to me. They chase petty-larceny cases and kick in doors. I wouldn't stoop to what they do. It's being mixed up the way I am with the problems of two governments that catches me." He added magnanimously, "You see something of that yourself."

We left the ship at Brooklyn, and with regret I prepared to bid Schnitzel farewell. Seldom had I met a little beast so offensive, but his vanity, his lies, his moral blindness, made one pity him. And in ten days in the smoking-room together we had had many friendly drinks and many friendly laughs. He was going to a hotel on lower Broadway, and as my cab, on my way uptown, passed the door, I offered him a lift. He appeared to consider the advisability of this, and then, with much by-play of glancing over his shoulder, dived into the front seat and drew down the blinds. "This hotel I am going to is an old-fashioned trap," he explained, "but the clerk is wise to me, understand, and I don't have to sign the register."

As we drew nearer to the hotel, he said: "It's a pity we can't dine out somewheres and go to the theatre, but—you know?"

With almost too much heartiness I hastily agreed it would be imprudent.

"I understand perfectly," I assented. "You are a marked man. Until you get those papers safe in the hands of your 'people,' you must be very cautious."

"That's right," he said. Then he smiled craftily.

"I wonder if you're on yet to which my people are."

I assured him that I had no idea, but that from the avidity with which he had abused them I guessed he was working for the Walker-Keefe crowd.

He both smiled and scowled.

"Don't you wish you knew?" he said. "I've told you a lot of inside stories, Mr. Crosby, but I'll never tell on my pals again. Not me! That's *my* secret."

At the door of the hotel he bade me a hasty good-by, and for a few minutes I believed that Schnitzel had passed out of my life forever. Then, in taking account of my belongings, I missed my field-glasses. I remembered that, in order to open a trunk for the customs inspectors, I had handed them to Schnitzel, and that he had hung them over his shoulder. In our haste at parting we both had forgotten them.

I was only a few blocks from the hotel, and I told the man to return.

I inquired for Mr. Schnitzel, and the clerk, who apparently knew him by that name, said he was in his room, number eighty-two.

"But he has a caller with him now," he added. "A gentleman was waiting for him, and's just gone up."

I wrote on my card why I had called, and soon after it had been borne skyward the clerk said:

"I guess he'll be able to see you now. That's the party that was calling on him, there."

He nodded toward a man who crossed the rotunda quickly. His face was twisted from us, as though, as he almost ran toward the street, he were reading the advertisements on the wall.

He reached the door, and was lost in the great tide of Broadway.

I crossed to the elevator, and as I stood waiting, it descended with a crash, and the boy who had taken my card flung himself, shrieking, into the rotunda.

"That man—stop him!" he cried. "The man in eighty-two—he's murdered."

The clerk vaulted the desk and sprang into the street, and I dragged the boy back to the wire rope and we shot to the third story. The boy shrank back. A chambermaid, crouching against the wall, her face colorless, lowered one hand, and pointed at an open door.

"In there," she whispered.

In a mean, common room, stretched where he had been struck back upon the bed, I found the boy who had elected to meddle in the "problems of two governments."

In tiny jets, from three wide knife-wounds, his blood flowed slowly. His staring eyes were lifted up in fear and in entreaty. I knew that he was dying, and as I felt my impotence to help him, I as keenly felt a great rage and a hatred toward those who had struck him.

I leaned over him until my eyes were only a few inches from his face.

"Schnitzel!" I cried. "Who did this? You can trust me. Who did this? Quick!"

I saw that he recognized me, and that there was something which, with terrible effort, he was trying to make me understand.

In the hall was the rush of many people, running, exclaiming, the noise of bells ringing; from another floor the voice of a woman shrieked hysterically.

At the sounds the eyes of the boy grew eloquent with entreaty, and with a movement that called from each wound a fresh outburst, like a man strangling, he lifted his fingers to his throat.

Voices were calling for water, to wait for the doctor, to wait for the police. But I thought I understood.

Still doubting him, still unbelieving, ashamed of my own credulity, I tore at his collar, and my fingers closed upon a package of oiled silk.

I stooped, and with my teeth ripped it open, and holding before him the slips of paper it contained, tore them into tiny shreds.

The eyes smiled at me with cunning, with triumph, with deep content.

It was so like the Schnitzel I had known that I believed still he might have strength enough to help me.

"Who did this?" I begged. "I'll hang him for it! Do you hear me?" I cried.

Seeing him lying there, with the life cut out of him, swept me with a blind anger, with a need to punish.

"I'll see they hang for it. Tell me!" I commanded. "Who did this?"

The eyes, now filled with weariness, looked up and the lips moved feebly.

"My own people," he whispered.

In my indignation I could have shaken the truth from him. I bent closer.

"Then, by God," I whispered back, "you'll tell me who they are!"

The eyes flashed sullenly.

"That's my secret," said Schnitzel.

The eyes set and the lips closed.

A man at my side leaned over him, and drew the sheet across his face.

# THE MESSENGERS

WHEN Ainsley first moved to Lone Lake Farm all of his friends asked him the same question. They wanted to know, if the farmer who sold it to him had abandoned it as worthless, how one of the idle rich, who could not distinguish a plough from a harrow, hoped to make it pay. His answer was that he had not purchased the farm as a means of getting richer by honest toil, but as a retreat from the world and as a test of true friendship. He argued that the people he knew accepted his hospitality at Sherry's because, in any event, they themselves would be dining within a taxicab fare of the same place. But if to see him they travelled all the way to Lone Lake Farm, he might feel assured that they were friends indeed.

Lone Lake Farm was spread over many acres of rocky ravine and forest, at a point where Connecticut approaches New York, and between it and the nearest railroad station stretched six miles of an execrable wood road. In this wilderness, directly upon the lonely lake, and at a spot equally distant from each of his boundary lines, Ainsley built himself a red brick house. Here, in solitude, he exiled himself; ostensibly to become a gentleman farmer; in reality to wait until Polly Kirkland had made up her mind to marry him.

Lone Lake, which gave the farm its name, was a pond hardly larger than a city block. It was fed by hidden springs, and fringed about with reeds and cat-tails, stunted willows and shivering birch. From its surface jutted points of the same rock that had made farming unremunerative, and to these miniature promontories and islands Ainsley, in keeping with a fancied resemblance, gave such names as the Needles, St. Helena, the Isle of Pines. From the edge of the pond that was farther from the house rose a high hill, heavily wooded. At its base, oak and chestnut trees spread their branches over the water, and when the air was still were so clearly reflected in the pond that the leaves seemed to float upon the surface. To the smiling expanse of the farm the lake was what the eye is to the human countenance. The oaks were its eyebrows, the fringe of reeds its lashes, and, in changing mood, it flashed with happiness or brooded in sombre melancholy. For Ainsley it held a deep attraction. Through the summer evenings, as the sun set, he would sit on the brick terrace and watch the fish leaping, and listen to the venerable bull-frogs croaking false alarms of rain. Indeed, after he met Polly Kirkland, staring moodily at the lake became his favorite form of exercise. With a number of other men, Ainsley was very much in love with Miss Kirkland, and unprejudiced friends thought that if she were to choose any of her devotees, Ainsley should be that one. Ainsley heartily agreed in this opinion, but in persuading Miss Kirkland to share it he had not been successful. This was partly his own fault; for when he dared to compare what she meant to him with what he had to offer her he became a mass of sodden humility. Could he have known how much Polly Kirkland envied and admired his depth of feeling, entirely apart from the fact that she herself inspired that feeling, how greatly she wished to care for him in the way he cared for her, life, even alone in the silences of Lone Lake, would have been a beautiful and blessed thing. But he was so sure she was the most charming and most wonderful girl in all the world, and he an unworthy and despicable being, that when the lady demurred, he faltered, and his pleading, at least to his own ears, carried no conviction.

"When one thinks of being married," said Polly Kirkland gently, "it isn't a question of the man you can live with, but the man you can't live without. And I am sorry, but I've not found that man."

"I suppose," returned Ainsley gloomily, "that my not being able to live without you doesn't affect the question in the least?"

"You *have* lived without me," Miss Kirkland pointed out reproachfully, "for thirty years."

"Lived!" almost shouted Ainsley. "Do you call *that* living? What was I before I met you? I was an ignorant beast of the field. I knew as much about living as one of the cows on my farm. I could sleep twelve hours at a stretch, or, if I was in New York, I *never* slept. I was a Day and Night Bank of health and happiness, a great, big, useless puppy. And now I can't sleep, can't eat, can't think—except of you. I dream about you all night, think about you all day, go through the woods calling your name, cutting your initials in tree trunks, doing all the fool things a man does when he's in love, and I am the most miserable man in the world— and the happiest!"

He finally succeeded in making Miss Kirkland so miserable also that she decided to run away. Friends had planned to spend the early spring on the Nile and were eager that she should accompany them. To her the separation seemed to offer an excellent method of discovering whether or not Ainsley was the man she could not "live without."

Ainsley saw in it only an act of torture, devised with devilish cruelty.

"What will happen to me," he announced firmly, "is that I will plain *die!* As long as I can see you, as long as I have the chance to try and make you understand that no one can possibly love you as I do, and as long as I know I am worrying you to death, and no one else is, I still hope. I've no right to hope, still I do. And that one little chance keeps me alive. But Egypt! If you escape to Egypt, what hold will I have on you? You might as well be in the moon. Can you imagine me writing love-letters to a woman in the moon? Can I send American Beauty roses to the ruins of Karnak? Here I can telephone you; not that I ever have anything to say that you want to hear, but because I want to listen to your voice, and to have you ask, 'Oh! is that *you?*' as though you were glad it *was* me. But Egypt! Can I call up Egypt on the long-distance? If you leave me now, you'll leave me forever, for I'll drown myself in Lone Lake."

The day she sailed away he went to the steamer, and, separating her from her friends and family, drew her to the side of the ship farther from the wharf, and which for the moment, was deserted. Directly below a pile-driver, with rattling of chains and shrieks from her donkey-engine, was smashing great logs; on the deck above, the ship's band was braying forth fictitious gayety, and from every side they were assailed by the raucous whistles of ferry-boats. The surroundings were not conducive to sentiment, but for the first time Polly Kirkland seemed a little uncertain, a little frightened; almost on the verge of tears, almost persuaded to surrender. For the first time she laid her hand on Ainsley's arm, and the shock sent the blood to his heart and held him breathless. When the girl looked at him there was something in her eyes that neither he nor any other man had ever seen there.

"The last thing I tell you," she said, "the thing I want you to remember, is this, that, though I do not care—I *want* to care."

Ainsley caught at her hand and, to the delight of the crew of a passing tug-boat, kissed it rapturously. His face was radiant. The fact of parting from her had caused him real suffering, had marked his face with hard lines. Now, hope and happiness smoothed them away and his eyes shone with his love for her. He was trembling, laughing, jubilant.

"And if you should!" he begged. "How soon will I know? You will cable," he commanded.

"You will cable 'Come,' and the same hour I'll start toward you. I'll go home now," he cried, "and pack!"

The girl drew away. Already she regretted the admission she had made. In fairness and in kindness to him she tried to regain the position she had abandoned.

"But a change like that," she pleaded, "might not come for years, may never come!" To recover herself, to make the words she had uttered seem less serious, she spoke quickly and lightly.

"And how could I *cable* such a thing!" she protested. "It would be far too sacred, too precious. You should be able to *feel* that the change has come."

"I suppose I should," assented Ainsley, doubtfully; "but it's a long way across two oceans. It would be safer if you'd promise to use the cable. Just one word: 'Come.'"

The girl shook her head and frowned.

"If you can't feel that the woman you love loves you, even across the world, you cannot love her very deeply."

"I don't have to answer that!" said Ainsley.

"I will send you a sign," continued the girl, hastily; "a secret wireless message. It shall be a test. If you love me you will read it at once. You will know the instant you see it that it comes from me. No one else will be able to read it; but if you love me, you will know that I love you."

Whether she spoke in metaphor or in fact, whether she was "playing for time," or whether in her heart she already intended to soon reward him with a message of glad tidings, Ainsley could not decide. And even as he begged her to enlighten him the last whistle blew, and a determined officer ordered him to the ship's side.

"Just as in everything that is beautiful," he whispered eagerly, "I always see something of you, so now in everything wonderful I will read your message. But," he persisted, "how shall I be *sure?*"

The last bag of mail had shot into the hold, the most reluctant of the visitors were being hustled down the last remaining gangplank. Ainsley's state was desperate.

"Will it be in symbol, or in cipher?" he demanded. "Must I read it in the sky, or will you hide it in a letter, or—where? Help me! Give me just a hint!"

The girl shook her head.

"You will read it—in your heart," she said.

From the end of the wharf Ainsley watched the funnels of the ship disappear in the haze of the lower bay. His heart was sore and heavy,

but in it there was still room for righteous indignation. "Read it in my heart!" he protested.
"How the devil can I read it in my heart? I
want to read it *printed* in a cablegram."

Because he had always understood that young
men in love found solace for their misery in
solitude and in communion with nature, he at
once drove his car to Lone Lake. But his
misery was quite genuine, and the emptiness
of the brick house only served to increase his
loneliness. He had built the house for her,
though she had never visited it, and was associated with it only through the somewhat
indefinite medium of the telephone box. But
in New York they had been much together.
And Ainsley quickly decided that in revisiting
those places where he had been happy in her
company he would derive from the recollection
some melancholy consolation. He accordingly
raced back through the night to the city; nor
did he halt until he was at the door of her house.
She had left it only that morning, and though
it was locked in darkness, it still spoke of her.
At least it seemed to bring her nearer to him
than when he was listening to the frogs in the
lake, and crushing his way through the pines.

He was not hungry, but he went to a restaurant where, when he was host, she had often
been the honored guest, and he pretended they

were at supper together and without a chaperon.
Either the illusion, or the supper cheered him,
for he was encouraged to go on to his club.
There in the library, with the aid of an atlas,
he worked out where, after thirteen hours of
moving at the rate of twenty-two knots an
hour, she should be at that moment. Having
determined that fact to his own satisfaction,
he sent a wireless after the ship. It read: "It
is now midnight and you are in latitude 40°
north, longitude 68° west, and I have grown
old and gray waiting for the sign."

The next morning, and for many days after,
he was surprised to find that the city went on
as though she still were in it. With unfeeling
regularity the sun rose out of the East River.
On Broadway electric-light signs flashed, street-
cars pursued each other, taxicabs bumped and
skidded, women, and even men, dared to look
happy, and had apparently taken some thought
to their attire. They did not respect even his
widowerhood. They smiled upon him, and
asked him jocularly about the farm and his
"crops," and what he was doing in New York.
He pitied them, for obviously they were ignorant
of the fact that in New York there were art
galleries, shops, restaurants of great interest,
owing to the fact that Polly Kirkland had
visited them. They did not know that on

upper Fifth Avenue were houses of which she had deigned to approve, or which she had destroyed with ridicule, and that to walk that avenue and halt before each of these houses was an inestimable privilege.

Each day, with pathetic vigilance, Ainsley examined his heart for the promised sign. But so far from telling him that the change he longed for had taken place, his heart grew heavier, and as weeks went by and no sign appeared, what little confidence he had once enjoyed passed with them.

But before hope entirely died, several false alarms had thrilled him with happiness. One was a cablegram from Gibraltar in which the only words that were intelligible were "congratulate" and "engagement." This lifted him into an ecstasy of joy and excitement, until, on having the cable company repeat the message, he learned it was a request from Miss Kirkland to congratulate two mutual friends who had just announced their engagement, and of whose address she was uncertain. He had hardly recovered from this disappointment than he was again thrown into a tumult by the receipt of a mysterious package from the custom-house containing an intaglio ring. The ring came from Italy, and her ship had touched at Genoa. The fact that it was addressed in an unknown handwriting did not disconcert him, for he argued that to make the test more difficult she might disguise the handwriting. He at once carried the intaglio to an expert at the Metropolitan Museum, and when he was told that it represented Cupid feeding a fire upon an altar, he reserved a stateroom on the first steamer bound for the Mediterranean. But before his ship sailed, a letter, also from Italy, from his Aunt Maria, who was spending the winter in Rome, informed him that the ring was a Christmas gift from her. In his rage he unjustly condemned Aunt Maria as a meddling old busybody, and gave her ring to the cook.

After two months of pilgrimages to places sacred to the memory of Polly Kirkland, Ainsley found that feeding his love on post-mortems was poor fare, and, in surrender, determined to evacuate New York. Since her departure he had received from Miss Kirkland several letters, but they contained no hint of a change in her affections, and search them as he might, he could find no cipher or hidden message. They were merely frank, friendly notes of travel; at first filled with gossip of the steamer, and later telling of excursions around Cairo. If they held any touch of feeling they seemed to show that she was sorry for him, and as she could not regard him in any way more calculated to increase his discouragement, he, in utter hopelessness, retreated to the solitude of the farm. In New York he left behind him two trunks filled with such garments as a man would need on board a steamer and in the early spring in Egypt. They had been packed and in readiness since the day she sailed away, when she had told him of the possible sign. But there had been no sign. Nor did he longer believe in one. So in the baggage-room of a hotel the trunks were abandoned, accumulating layers of dust and charges for storage.

At the farm the snow still lay in the crevices of the rocks and beneath the branches of the evergreens, but under the wet, dead leaves little flowers had begun to show their faces. The "backbone of the winter was broken" and spring was in the air. But as Ainsley was certain that his heart also was broken, the signs of spring did not console him. At each week-end he filled the house with people, but they found him gloomy and he found them dull. He liked better the solitude of the midweek days. Then for hours he would tramp through the woods, pretending she was at his side, pretending he was helping her across the streams swollen with winter rains and melted snow. On these excursions he cut down trees that hid a view he thought she would have liked, he cut paths over which she might have walked. Or he sat idly in a flat-bottomed scow in the lake and made a pretense of fishing. The loneliness of the lake and the isolation of the boat suited his humor. He did not find it true that misery loves company. At least to human beings he preferred his companions of Lone Lake—the beaver building his home among the reeds, the kingfisher, the blue heron, the wild fowl that in their flight north rested for an hour or a day upon the peaceful waters. He looked upon them as his guests, and when they spread their wings and left him again alone he felt he had been hardly used.

It was while he was sunk in this state of melancholy, and some months after Miss Kirkland had sailed to Egypt, that hope returned.

For a week-end he had invited Holden and Lowell, two former classmates, and Nelson Mortimer and his bride. They were all old friends of their host and well acquainted with the cause of his discouragement. So they did not ask to be entertained, but, disregarding him, amused themselves after their own fashion. It was late Friday afternoon. The members of the house-party had just returned from a tramp through the woods and had joined Ainsley on the terrace, where he stood watching the last rays of the sun leave the lake in darkness. All through the day there had been sharp splashes of rain with the clouds dull and forbidding, but now the sun was sinking in a sky of crimson, and for the morrow a faint moon held out a promise of fair weather.

Elsie Mortimer gave a sudden exclamation, and pointed to the east. "Look!" she said.

The men turned and followed the direction of her hand. In the fading light, against a background of sombre clouds that the sun could not reach, they saw, moving slowly toward them and descending as they moved, six great white birds. When they were above the tops of the trees that edged the lake, the birds halted and hovered uncertainly, their wings lifting and falling, their bodies slanting and sweeping slowly, in short circles.

The suddenness of their approach, their presence so far inland, something unfamiliar and foreign in the way they had winged their progress, for a moment held the group upon the terrace silent.

"They are gulls from the Sound," said Lowell.

"They are too large for gulls," returned Mortimer. "They might be wild geese, but," he answered himself, in a puzzled voice, "it is too late; and wild geese follow a leader."

As though they feared the birds might hear

them and take alarm, the men, unconsciously had spoken in low tones.

"They move as though they were very tired," whispered Elsie Mortimer.

"I think," said Ainsley, "they have lost their way."

But even as he spoke, the birds, as though they had reached their goal, spread their wings to the full length and sank to the shallow water at the farthest margin of the lake.

As they fell the sun struck full upon them, turning their great pinions into flashing white and silver.

"Oh!" cried the girl, "but they are beautiful!"

Between the house and the lake there was a ridge of rock higher than the head of a man, and to this Ainsley and his guests ran for cover. On hands and knees, like hunters stalking game, they scrambled up the face of the rock and peered cautiously into the pond. Below them, less than one hundred yards away, on a tiny promontory, the six white birds stood motionless. They showed no sign of fear. They could not but know that beyond the lonely circle of the pond were the haunts of men. From the farm came the tinkle of a cow-bell, the bark of a dog, and in the valley, six miles distant, rose faintly upon the stillness of the

"I think," said Ainsley, "they have lost their way."

sunset hour the rumble of a passing train. But if these sounds carried, the birds gave no heed. In each drooping head and dragging wing, in the forward stoop of each white body, weighing heavily on the slim, black legs, was written utter weariness, abject fatigue. To each even to lower his bill and sip from the cool waters was a supreme effort. And in their exhaustion so complete was something humanly helpless and pathetic.

To Ainsley the mysterious visitors made a direct appeal. He felt as though they had thrown themselves upon his hospitality. That they showed such confidence that the sanctuary would be kept sacred touched him. And while his friends spoke eagerly, he remained silent, watching the drooping, ghost-like figures, his eyes filled with pity.

"I have seen birds like those in Florida," Mortimer was whispering, "but they were not migratory birds."

"And I've seen white cranes in the Adirondacks," said Lowell, "but never six at one time."

"They're like no bird *I* ever saw out of a zoo," declared Elsie Mortimer. "Maybe they are from the Zoo? Maybe they escaped from the Bronx?"

"The Bronx is too near," objected Lowell.

"These birds have come a great distance. They move as though they had been flying for many days."

As though the absurdity of his own thought amused him, Mortimer laughed softly.

"I'll tell you what they *do* look like," he said. "They look like that bird you see on the Nile, the sacred Ibis, they——"

Something between a gasp and a cry startled him into silence. He found his host staring wildly, his lips parted, his eyes open wide.

"Where?" demanded Ainsley. "Where did you say?" His voice was so hoarse, so strange, that they all turned and looked.

"On the Nile," repeated Mortimer. "All over Egypt. Why?"

Ainsley made no answer. Unclasping his hold, he suddenly slid down the face of the rock, and with a bump lit on his hands and knees. With one bound he had cleared a flower-bed. In two more he had mounted the steps to the terrace, and in another instant had disappeared into the house.

"What happened to him?" demanded Elsie Mortimer.

"He's gone to get a gun!" exclaimed Mortimer. "But he mustn't! How can he think of shooting them?" he cried indignantly. "I'll put a stop to that!"

# THE MESSENGERS

In the hall he found Ainsley surrounded by a group of startled servants.

"You get that car at the door in five minutes!" he was shouting, "and *you* telephone the hotel to have my trunks out of the cellar and on board the *Kron Prinz Albert* by midnight. Then you telephone Hoboken that I want a cabin, and if they haven't got a cabin I want the captain's. And tell them anyway I'm coming on board to-night, and I'm going with them if I have to sleep on deck. And *you*," he cried, turning to Mortimer, "take a shotgun and guard that lake, and if anybody tries to molest those birds—shoot him! They've come from Egypt! From Polly Kirkland! She sent them! They're a sign!"

"Are you going mad?" cried Mortimer.

"No!" roared Ainsley. "I'm going to Egypt, and I'm going *now!*"

Polly Kirkland and her friends were travelling slowly up the Nile, and had reached Luxor. A few hundred yards below the village their dahabiyeh was moored to the bank, and, on the deck, Miss Kirkland was watching a scarlet sun sink behind two palm-trees. By the grace of that special Providence that cares for drunken men, citizens of the United States, and lovers, her friends were on shore, and she was alone. For this she was grateful, for her thoughts were of a melancholy and tender nature and she had no wish for any companion save one. In consequence, when a steam-launch, approaching at full speed with the rattle of a quick-firing gun, broke upon her meditations, she was distinctly annoyed.

But when, with much ringing of bells and shouting of orders, the steam-launch rammed the paint off her dahabiyeh, and a young man flung himself over the rail and ran toward her, her annoyance passed, and with a sigh she sank into his outstretched, eager arms.

Half an hour later Ainsley laughed proudly and happily.

"Well!" he exclaimed, "you can never say I kept *you* waiting. I didn't lose much time, did I? Ten minutes after I got your C. Q. D. signal I was going down the Boston Post Road at seventy miles an hour."

"My what?" said the girl.

"The sign!" explained Ainsley. "The sign you were to send me to tell me"—he bent over her hands and added gently—"that you cared for me."

"Oh, I remember," laughed Polly Kirkland. "I was to send you a sign, wasn't I? You were to 'read it in your heart,'" she quoted.

"And I did," returned Ainsley complacently. "There were several false alarms, and I'd almost lost hope, but when the messengers came I knew them."

With puzzled eyes the girl frowned and raised her head.

"Messengers?" she repeated. "I sent no message. Of course," she went on, "when I said you would 'read it in your heart' I meant that if you *really* loved me you would not wait for a sign, but you would just *come!*" She sighed proudly and contentedly. "And you came. You understood that, didn't you?" she asked anxiously.

For an instant Ainsley stared blankly, and then to hide his guilty countenance drew her toward him and kissed her.

"Of course," he stammered—"of course I understood. That was why I came. I just couldn't stand it any longer."

Breathing heavily at the thought of the blunder he had so narrowly avoided, Ainsley turned his head toward the great red disk that was disappearing into the sands of the desert. He was so long silent that the girl lifted her eyes, and found that already he had forgotten her presence and, transfixed, was staring at the sky. On his face was bewilderment and wonder and a touch of awe. The girl followed the direction of his eyes, and in the swiftly gathering darkness saw coming slowly toward them, and descending as they came, six great white birds.

They moved with the last effort of complete exhaustion. In the drooping head and dragging wings of each was written utter weariness, abject fatigue. For a moment they hovered over the dahabiyeh and above the two young lovers, and then, like tired travellers who had reached their journey's end, they spread their wings and sank to the muddy waters of the Nile and into the enveloping night.

"Some day," said Ainsley, "I have a confession to make to you."

# A WASTED DAY

When its turn came, the private secretary, somewhat apologetically, laid the letter in front of the Wisest Man in Wall Street.

"From Mrs. Austin, probation officer, Court of General Sessions," he explained. "Wants a letter about Spear. He's been convicted of theft. Comes up for sentence Tuesday."

"Spear?" repeated Arnold Thorndike.

"Young fellow, stenographer, used to do your letters last summer going in and out on the train."

The great man nodded. "I remember. What about him?"

The habitual gloom of the private secretary was lightened by a grin.

"Went on the loose; had with him about five hundred dollars belonging to the firm; he's with Isaacs & Sons now, shoe people on Sixth Avenue. Met a woman, and woke up without the money. The next morning he offered to make good, but Isaacs called in a policeman. When they looked into it, they found the boy had been drunk. They tried to withdraw the charge, but he'd been committed. Now, the probation officer is trying to get the judge to suspend sentence. A letter from you, sir, would——"

It was evident the mind of the great man was elsewhere. Young men who, drunk or sober, spent the firm's money on women who disappeared before sunrise did not appeal to him. Another letter submitted that morning had come from his art agent in Europe. In Florence he had discovered the Correggio he had been sent to find. It was undoubtedly genuine, and he asked to be instructed by cable. The price was forty thousand dollars. With one eye closed, and the other keenly regarding the inkstand, Mr. Thorndike decided to pay the price; and with the facility of long practise dismissed the Correggio, and snapped his mind back to the present.

"Spear had a letter from us when he left, didn't he?" he asked. "What he has developed into, *since* he left us—" he shrugged his shoulders. The secretary withdrew the letter, and slipped another in its place.

"Homer Firth, the landscape man," he chanted, "wants permission to use blue flint on the new road, with turf gutters, and to plant silver firs each side. Says it will run to about five thousand dollars a mile."

"No!" protested the great man firmly, "blue flint makes a country place look like a cemetery. Mine looks too much like a cemetery now. Landscape gardeners!" he exclaimed impatiently. "Their only idea is to insult nature. The place was better the day I bought it, when it was running wild; you could pick flowers all the way to the gates." Pleased that it should have recurred to him, the great man smiled. "Why, Spear," he exclaimed, "always took in a bunch of them for his mother. Don't you remember, we used to see him before breakfast wandering around the grounds picking flowers?" Mr. Thorndike nodded briskly. "I like his taking flowers to his mother."

"He *said* it was to his mother," suggested the secretary gloomily.

"Well, he picked the flowers, anyway," laughed Mr. Thorndike. "He didn't pick our pockets. And he had the run of the house in those days. As far as we know," he dictated, "he was satisfactory. Don't say more than that."

The secretary scribbled a mark with his pencil. "And the landscape man?"

"Tell him," commanded Thorndike, "I want a wood road, suitable to a farm; and to let the trees grow where God planted them."

As his car slid downtown on Tuesday morning the mind of Arnold Thorndike was occupied with such details of daily routine as the purchase of a railroad, the Japanese loan, the new wing to his art gallery, and an attack that morning, in his own newspaper, upon his pet trust. But his busy mind was not too occupied to return the salutes of the traffic policemen who cleared the way for him. Or, by some genius of memory, to recall the fact that it was on this morning young Spear was to be sentenced for theft. It was a charming morning. The spring was at full tide, and the air was sweet and clean. Mr. Thorndike considered whimsically that to send a man to jail with the memory of such a morning clinging to him was adding a year to his sentence. He regretted he had not given the probation officer a stronger letter. He remembered the young man now, and favorably. A shy, silent youth, deft in work, and at other times conscious and embarrassed. But that, on the part of a stenographer, in the presence of the Wisest Man in Wall Street, was not unnatural. On occasions, Mr. Thorndike had put even royalty—frayed, impecunious royalty, on the lookout for a loan—at its ease.

The hood of the car was down, and the taste of the air, warmed by the sun, was grateful. It was at this time, a year before, that young Spear picked the spring flowers to take to his mother. A year from now where would young Spear be?

# A WASTED DAY

It was characteristic of the great man to act quickly, so quickly that his friends declared he was a slave to impulse. It was these same impulses, leading so invariably to success, that made his enemies call him the Wisest Man. He leaned forward and touched the chauffeur's shoulder. "Stop at the Court of General Sessions," he commanded. What he proposed to do would take but a few minutes. A word, a personal word from him to the district attorney, or the judge, would be enough. He recalled that a Sunday Special had once calculated that the working time of Arnold Thorndike brought him in two hundred dollars a minute. At that rate, keeping Spear out of prison would cost a thousand dollars.

Out of the sunshine Mr. Thorndike stepped into the gloom of an echoing rotunda, shut in on every side, hung by balconies, lit, many stories overhead, by a dirty skylight. The place was damp, the air acrid with the smell of stale tobacco juice, and foul with the presence of many unwashed humans. A policeman, chewing stolidly, nodded toward an elevator shaft, and other policemen nodded him further on to the office of the district attorney. There Arnold Thorndike breathed more freely. He was again among his own people. He could not help but appreciate the dramatic qualities of the situation; that the richest man in Wall Street should appear in person to plead for a humble and weaker brother. He knew he could not escape recognition, his face was too well known, but, he trusted, for the sake of Spear, the reporters would make no display of his visit. With a deprecatory laugh, he explained why he had come. But the outburst of appropbation he had anticipated did not follow.

The district attorney ran his finger briskly down a printed card. "Henry Spear," he exclaimed, "that's your man. Part Three, Judge Fallon. Andrews is in that court." He walked to the door of his private office. "Andrews!" he called.

He introduced an alert, broad-shouldered young man of years of much indiscretion and with a charming and inconsequent manner.

"Mr. Thorndike is interested in Henry Spear, coming up for sentence in Part Three this morning. Wants to speak for him. Take him over with you."

The district attorney shook hands quickly, and retreated to his private office. Mr. Andrews took out a cigarette and, as he crossed the floor, lit it.

"Come with me," he commanded. Somewhat puzzled, slightly annoyed, but enjoying

withal the novelty of the environment and the
curtness of his reception, Mr. Thorndike followed. He decided that, in his ignorance, he
had wasted his own time and that of the pros-
ecuting attorney. He should at once have sent
in his card to the judge. As he understood
it, Mr. Andrews was now conducting him to
that dignitary, and, in a moment, he would be
free to return to his own affairs, which were the
affairs of two continents. But Mr. Andrews
led him to an office, bare and small, and offered
him a chair, and handed him a morning newspaper. There were people waiting in the room;
strange people, only like those Mr. Thorndike
had seen on ferry-boats. They leaned forward
toward young Mr. Andrews, fawning, their eyes
wide with apprehension.

Mr. Thorndike refused the newspaper. "I
thought I was going to see the judge," he
suggested.

"Court doesn't open for a few minutes yet,"
said the assistant district attorney. "Judge is
always late, anyway."

Mr. Thorndike suppressed an exclamation.
He wanted to protest, but his clear mind showed
him that there was nothing against which, with
reason, he could protest. He could not com-
plain because these people were not apparently
aware of the sacrifice he was making. He had

come among them to perform a kindly act.
He recognized that he must not stultify it by a
show of irritation. He had precipitated himself into a game of which he did not know the
rules. That was all. Next time he would know
better. Next time he would send a clerk. But
he was not without a sense of humor, and the
situation as it now was forced upon him struck
him as amusing. He laughed good-naturedly
and reached for the desk telephone.

"May I use this?" he asked. He spoke to
the Wall Street office. He explained he would
be a few minutes late. He directed what should
be done if the market opened in a certain way.
He gave rapid orders on many different matters,
asked to have read to him a cablegram he
expected from Petersburg, and one from Vienna.

"They answer each other," was his final
instruction. "It looks like peace."

Mr. Andrews with genial patience had remained silent. Now he turned upon his visitors.
A Levantine, burly, unshaven, and soiled,
towered truculently above him. Young Mr.
Andrews with his swivel chair tilted back, his
hands clasped behind his head, his cigarette
hanging from his lips, regarded the man dis-
passionately.

"You gotta hell of a nerve to come to see me,"
he commented cheerfully. To Mr. Thorndike,

the form of greeting was novel. So greatly did
it differ from the procedure of his own office,
that he listened with interest.

"Was it you," demanded young Andrews, in a
puzzled tone, "or your brother who tried to
knife me?" Mr. Thorndike, unaccustomed to
cross the pavement to his office unless escorted
by bank messengers and plain-clothes men,
felt the room growing rapidly smaller; the figure
of the truculent Greek loomed to heroic pro-
portions. The hand of the banker went vaguely
to his chin, and from there fell to his pearl pin,
which he hastily covered.

"Get out!" said young Andrews, "and don't
show your face here——"

The door slammed upon the flying Greek.
Young Andrews swung his swivel chair so that,
over his shoulder, he could see Mr. Thorndike.
"I don't like his face," he explained.

A kindly eyed, sad woman with a basket on
her knee smiled upon Andrews with the famili-
arity of an old acquaintance.

"Is that woman going to get a divorce from
my son," she asked, "now that he's in trouble?"

"Now that he's in Sing Sing?" corrected Mr.
Andrews. "I *hope* so! She deserves it. That
son of yours, Mrs. Bernard," he declared em-
phatically, "is no good!"

The brutality shocked Mr. Thorndike. For

the woman he felt a thrill of sympathy, but at once saw that it was superfluous. From the secure and lofty heights of motherhood, Mrs. Bernard smiled down upon the assistant district attorney as upon a naughty child. She did not even deign a protest. She continued merely to smile. The smile reminded Thorndike of the smile on the face of a mother in a painting by Murillo he had lately presented to the chapel in the college he had given to his native town.

"That son of yours," repeated young Andrews, "is a leech. He's robbed you, robbed his wife. Best thing I ever did for *you* was to send him up the river."

The mother smiled upon him beseechingly.

"Could you give me a pass?" she said.

Young Andrews flung up his hands and appealed to Thorndike.

"Isn't that just like a mother?" he protested. "That son of hers has broken her heart, tramped on her, cheated her; hasn't left her a cent; and she comes to me for a pass, so she can kiss him through the bars! And I'll bet she's got a cake for him in that basket!"

The mother laughed happily; she knew now she would get the pass.

"Mothers," explained Mr. Andrews, from the depth of his wisdom, "are all like that; your mother, my mother. If you went to jail, your mother would be just like that."

Mr. Thorndike bowed his head politely. He had never considered going to jail, or whether, if he did, his mother would bring him cake in a basket. Apparently there were many aspects and accidents of life not included in his experience.

Young Andrews sprang to his feet, and, with the force of a hose flushing a gutter, swept his soiled visitors into the hall.

"Come on," he called to the Wisest Man, "the court is open."

In the corridors were many people, and with his eyes on the broad shoulders of the assistant district attorney, Thorndike pushed his way through them. The people who blocked his progress were of the class unknown to him. Their looks were anxious, furtive, miserable. They stood in little groups, listening eagerly to a sharp-faced lawyer, or, in sullen despair, eying each other. At a door a tipstaff laid his hand roughly on the arm of Mr. Thorndike.

"That's all right, Joe," called young Mr. Andrews, "he's with *me*." They entered the court and passed down an aisle to a railed enclosure in which were high oak chairs. Again, in his effort to follow, Mr. Thorndike was halted, but the first tipstaff came to his rescue. "All right," he signalled, "he's with Mr. Andrews."

Mr. Andrews pointed to one of the oak chairs. "You sit there," he commanded, "it's reserved for members of the bar, but it's all right. You're with *me*."

Distinctly annoyed, slightly bewildered, the banker sank between the arms of a chair. He felt he had lost his individuality. Andrews had become his sponsor. Because of Andrews he was tolerated. Because Andrews had a pull he was permitted to sit as an equal among police-court lawyers. No longer was he Arnold Thorndike. He was merely the man "with Mr. Andrews."

Then even Andrews abandoned him. "The judge'll be here in a minute, now," said the assistant district attorney, and went inside a railed enclosure in front of the judge's bench. There he greeted another assistant district attorney whose years were those of even greater indiscretion than the years of Mr. Andrews. Seated on the rail, with their hands in their pockets and their backs turned to Mr. Thorndike, they laughed and talked together. The subject of their discourse was one Mike Donlin, as he appeared in vaudeville.

To Mr. Thorndike it was evident that young Andrews had entirely forgotten him. He arose, and touched his sleeve. With infinite sarcasm Mr. Thorndike began: "My engagements are not pressing, but——"

A court attendant beat with his palm upon the rail.

"Sit down!" whispered Andrews. "The judge is coming."

Mr. Thorndike sat down.

The court attendant droned loudly words Mr. Thorndike could not distinguish. There was a rustle of silk, and from a door behind him the judge stalked past. He was a young man, the type of the Tammany politician. On his shrewd, alert, Irish-American features was an expression of unnatural gloom. With a smile Mr. Thorndike observed that it was as little suited to the countenance of the young judge as was the robe to his shoulders. Mr. Thorndike was still smiling when young Andrews leaned over the rail.

"Stand up!" he hissed. Mr. Thorndike stood up.

After the court attendant had uttered more unintelligible words, every one sat down; and the financier again moved hurriedly to the rail.

"I would like to speak to him now before he begins," he whispered. "I can't wait."

Mr. Andrews stared in amazement. The

banker had not believed the young man could look so serious.

"Speak to him, *now!*" exclaimed the district attorney. "You've got to wait till your man comes up. If you speak to the judge, *now*—" The voice of Andrews faded away in horror.

Not knowing in what way he had offended, but convinced that it was only by the grace of Andrews he had escaped a dungeon, Mr. Thorndike retreated to his arm-chair.

The clock on the wall showed him that, already, he had given to young Spear one hour and a quarter. The idea was preposterous. No one better than himself knew what his time was really worth. In half an hour there was a board meeting; later, he was to hold a postmortem on a railroad; at every moment questions were being asked by telegraph, by cable, questions that involved the credit of individuals, of firms, of even the country. And the one man who could answer them was risking untold sums only that he might say a good word for an idle apprentice. Inside the railed enclosure a lawyer was reading a typewritten speech. He assured his honor that he must have more time to prepare his case. It was one of immense importance. The name of a most respectable business house was involved, and a sum of no less than nine hundred dollars. Nine hundred dollars! The contrast struck Mr. Thorndike's sense of humor full in the centre. Unknowingly, he laughed, and found himself as conspicuous as though he had appeared suddenly in his night-clothes. The tipstaffs beat upon the rail, the lawyer he had interrupted uttered an indignant exclamation, Andrews came hurriedly toward him, and the young judge slowly turned his head.

"Those persons," he said, "who cannot respect the dignity of this court will leave it." As he spoke, with his eyes fixed on those of Mr. Thorndike, the latter saw that the young judge had suddenly recognized him. But the fact of his identity did not cause the frown to relax or the rebuke to halt unuttered. In even, icy tones the judge continued: "And it is well they should remember that the law is no respecter of persons and that the dignity of this court will be enforced, no matter who the offender may happen to be."

Andrews slipped into the chair beside Mr. Thorndike, and grinned sympathetically.

"Sorry!" he whispered. "Should have warned you. We won't be long now," he added encouragingly. "As soon as this fellow finishes his argument, the judge'll take up the sentences. Your man seems to have other

friends; Isaacs & Sons are here, and the typewriter firm who taught him; but what *you* say
will help most. It won't be more than a couple
of hours now."

"A couple of hours!" Mr. Thorndike raged
inwardly. A couple of hours in this place where
he had been publicly humiliated. He smiled, a
thin, shark-like smile. Those who made it their
business to study his expressions, on seeing it,
would have fled. Young Andrews, not being
acquainted with the moods of the great man,
added cheerfully: "By one o'clock, anyway."

Mr. Thorndike began grimly to pull on his
gloves. For all he cared now young Spear could
go hang. Andrews nudged his elbow.

"See that old lady in the front row?" he whispered. "That's Mrs. Spear. What did I tell
you; mothers are all alike. She's not taken her
eyes off you since court opened. She knows
you're her one best bet."

Impatiently Mr. Thorndike raised his head.
He saw a little, white-haired woman who stared
at him. In her eyes was the same look he had
seen in the eyes of men who, at times of panic,
fled to him, beseeching, entreating, forcing upon
him what was left of the wreck of their fortunes,
if only he would save their honor.

"And here come the prisoners," Andrews whis-

pered. "See Spear? Third man from the last."
A long line, guarded in front and rear, shuffled
into the court-room, and, as ordered, ranged
themselves against the wall. Among them were
old men and young boys, well dressed, clever-
looking rascals, collarless tramps, fierce-eyed
aliens, smooth-shaven, thin-lipped Broadway-
ards—and Spear.

Spear, his head hanging, with lips white and
cheeks ashen, and his eyes heavy with shame.

Mr. Thorndike had risen, and, in farewell,
was holding out his hand to Andrews. He
turned, and across the court-room the eyes of
the financier and the stenographer met. At the
sight of the great man, Spear flushed crimson,
and then his look of despair slowly disappeared;
and into his eyes there came incredulously hope
and gratitude. He turned his head suddenly
to the wall.

Mr. Thorndike stood irresolute, and then sank
back into his chair.

The first man in the line was already at the
railing, and the questions put to him by the
judge were being repeated to him by the other
assistant district attorney and a court attendant. His muttered answers were in turn repeated to the judge.

"Says he's married, naturalized citizen, Lu-
theran Church, die-cutter by profession."

The probation officer, her hands filled with papers, bustled forward and whispered.

"Mrs. Austin says," continued the district attorney, "she's looked into this case, and asks to have the man turned over to her. He has a wife and three children; has supported them for five years."

"Is the wife in court?" the judge said.

A thin, washed-out, pretty woman stood up, and clasped her hands in front of her.

"Has this man been a good husband to you, madam?" asked the young judge.

The woman broke into vehement assurances. No man could have been a better husband. Would she take him back? Indeed she would take him back. She held out her hands as though she would physically drag her husband from the pillory.

The judge bowed toward the probation officer, and she beckoned the prisoner to her.

Other men followed, and in the fortune of each Mr. Thorndike found himself, to his surprise, taking a personal interest. It was as good as a play. It reminded him of the Sicilians he had seen in London in their little sordid tragedies. Only these actors were appearing in their proper persons in real dramas of a life he did not know, but which appealed to something that had been long untouched, long in disuse. It was an uncomfortable sensation that left him restless because, as he appreciated, it needed expression, an outlet. He found this, partially, in praising, through Andrews, the young judge who had publicly rebuked him. Mr. Thorndike found him astute, sane; his queries intelligent, his comments just. And this probation officer, she, too, was capable, was she not? Smiling at his interest in what to him was an old story, the younger man nodded.

"I like her looks," whispered the great man. "Like her clear eyes and clean skin. She strikes me as able, full of energy, and yet womanly. These men when they come under her charge," he insisted, eagerly, "need money to start again, don't they?" He spoke anxiously. He believed he had found the clew to his restlessness. It was a desire to help; to be of use to these failures who had fallen and who were being lifted to their feet. Andrews looked at him curiously. "Anything you give her," he answered, "would be well invested."

"If you will tell me her name and address?" whispered the banker. He was much given to charity, but it had been perfunctory, it was extended on the advice of his secretary. In helping here, he felt a genial glow of personal pleasure. It was much more satisfactory than giving an Old Master to his private chapel.

In the rear of the court-room there was a scuffle that caused every one to turn and look. A man, who had tried to force his way past the tipstaffs, was being violently ejected, and, as he disappeared, he waved a paper toward Mr. Thorndike. The banker recognized him as his chief clerk. Andrews rose anxiously. "That man wanted to get to you. I'll see what it is. Maybe it's important."

Mr. Thorndike pulled him back.

"Maybe it is," he said dryly. "But I can't see him now, I'm busy."

Slowly the long line of derelicts, of birds of prey, of sorry, weak failures, passed before the seat of judgment. Mr. Thorndike had moved into a chair nearer to the rail, and from time to time made a note upon the back of an envelope. He had forgotten the time or had chosen to disregard it. So great was his interest that he had forgotten the particular derelict he had come to serve, until Spear stood almost at his elbow.

Thorndike turned eagerly to the judge, and saw that he was listening to a rotund, gray little man with beady, bird-like eyes who, as he talked, bowed and gesticulated. Behind him stood a younger man, a more modern edition of the other. He also bowed and, behind gold eye-glasses, smiled ingratiatingly.

The judge nodded, and leaning forward, for a few moments fixed his eyes upon the prisoner. "You are a very fortunate young man," he said. He laid his hand upon a pile of letters. "When you were your own worst enemy, your friends came to help you. These letters speak for you; your employers, whom you robbed, have pleaded with me in your favor. It is urged, in your behalf, that at the time you committed the crime of which you are found guilty, you were intoxicated. In the eyes of the law, that is no excuse. Some men can drink and keep their senses. It appears you cannot. When you drink you are a menace to yourself— and, as is shown by this crime, to the community. Therefore, you must not drink. In view of the good character to which your friends have testified, and on the condition that you do not touch liquor, I will not sentence you to jail, but will place you in charge of the probation officer."

The judge leaned back in his chair and beckoned to Mr. Andrews. It was finished. Spear was free, and from different parts of the courtroom people were moving toward the door. Their numbers showed that the friends of the young man had been many. Mr. Thorndike felt a certain twinge of disappointment. Even though the result relieved and pleased him, he wished, in bringing it about, he had had some part.

He begrudged to Isaacs & Sons the credit of having given Spear his liberty. His morning had been wasted. He had neglected his own interests, and in no way assisted those of Spear. He was moving out of the railed enclosure when Andrews called him by name.

"His honor," he said impressively, "wishes to speak to you."

The judge leaned over his desk and shook Mr. Thorndike by the hand. Then he made a speech. The speech was about public-spirited citizens who, to the neglect of their own interests, came to assist the ends of justice, and fellow-creatures in misfortune. He purposely spoke in a loud voice, and every one stopped to listen.

"The law, Mr. Thorndike, is not vindictive," he said. "It wishes only to be just. Nor can it be swayed by wealth or political or social influences. But when there is good in a man, I, personally, want to know it, and when gentle-men like yourself, of your standing in this city, come here to speak a good word for a man, we would stultify the purpose of justice if we did not listen. I thank you for coming, and I wish more of our citizens were as unselfish and public-spirited."

It was all quite absurd and most embarrassing, but inwardly Mr. Thorndike glowed with plea-

sure. It was a long time since any one had had
the audacity to tell him he had done well.
From the friends of Spear there was a ripple of
applause, which no tipstaff took it upon himself
to suppress, and to the accompaniment of this,
Mr. Thorndike walked to the corridor. He was
pleased with himself and with his fellow-men.
He shook hands with Isaacs & Sons, and con-
gratulated them upon their public spirit, and
the typewriter firm upon their public spirit.
And then he saw Spear standing apart regarding
him doubtfully.

Spear did not offer his hand, but Mr. Thorndike took it, and shook it, and said: "I want
to meet your mother."

And when Mrs. Spear tried to stop sobbing
long enough to tell him how happy she was, and
how grateful, he instead told her what a fine son
she had, and that he remembered when Spear
used to carry flowers to town for her. And she
remembered it, too, and thanked him for the
flowers. And he told Spear, when Isaacs &
Sons went bankrupt, which at the rate they were
giving away their money to the Hebrew Hospital
would be very soon, Spear must come back to
him. And Isaacs & Sons were delighted at the
great man's pleasantry, and afterward repeated
it many times, calling upon each other to bear
witness, and Spear felt as though some one had
given him a new backbone, and Andrews, who

was guiding Thorndike out of the building, was thinking to himself what a great confidence man had been lost when Thorndike became a banker.

The chief clerk and two bank messengers were waiting by the automobile with written calls for help from the office. They pounced upon the banker and almost lifted him into the car.

"There's still time!" panted the chief clerk.

"There is not!" answered Mr. Thorndike. His tone was rebellious, defiant. It carried all the authority of a spoiled child of fortune. "I've wasted most of this day," he declared, "and I intend to waste the rest of it. Andrews," he called, "jump in, and I'll give you a lunch at Sherry's."

The vigilant protector of the public dashed back into the building.

"Wait till I get my hat!" he called.

As the two truants rolled up the avenue the spring sunshine warmed them, the sense of duties neglected added zest to their holiday, and young Mr. Andrews laughed aloud.

Mr. Thorndike raised his eyebrows inquiringly.

"I was wondering," said Andrews, "how much it cost you to keep Spear out of jail?"

"I don't care," said the great man guiltily; "it was worth it."

# A CHARMED LIFE

She loved him so, that when he went away to a little war in which his country was interested she could not understand, nor quite forgive.

As the correspondent of a newspaper, Chesterton had looked on at other wars; when the yellow races met, when the infidel Turk spanked the Christian Greek; and one he had watched from inside a British square, where he was greatly alarmed lest he should be trampled upon by terrified camels. This had happened before he and she had met. After they met, she told him that what chances he had chosen to take before he came into her life fell outside of her jurisdiction. But now that his life belonged to her, this talk of his standing up to be shot at was wicked. It was worse than wicked; it was absurd.

When the *Maine* sank in Havana harbor and the word "war" was appearing hourly in hysterical extras, Miss Armitage explained her position.

"You mustn't think," she said, "that I am one of those silly girls who would beg you not to go to war."

At the moment of speaking her cheek happened to be resting against his, and his arm was about her, so he humbly bent his head and kissed her, and whispered very proudly and softly, "No, dearest."

At which she withdrew from him frowning.

"No! I'm not a bit like those girls," she proclaimed. "I merely tell you *you can't go!* My gracious!" she cried, helplessly. She knew the words fell short of expressing her distress, but her education had not supplied her with exclamations of greater violence.

"My goodness!" she cried. "How can you frighten me so? It's not like you," she reproached him. "You are so unselfish, so noble. You are always thinking of other people. How can you talk of going to war—to be killed—to me? And now, now that you have made me love you so?"

The hands, that when she talked seemed to him like swallows darting and flashing in the sunlight, clutched his sleeve. The fingers, that he would rather kiss than the lips of any other woman that ever lived, clung to his arm. Their clasp reminded him of that of a drowning child he had once lifted from the surf.

"If you should die," whispered Miss Armitage, "what would I do! What would I do!"

"But, my dearest," cried the young man,

"My dearest one! I've *got* to go. It's our own war. Everybody else will go," he pleaded. "Every man you know, and they're going to fight, too. I'm going only to look on. That's bad enough, isn't it, without sitting at home? You should be sorry I'm not going to fight."

"Sorry!" exclaimed the girl. "If you love me——"

"If I love you," shouted the young man. His voice suggested that he was about to shake her. "How dare you?"

She abandoned that position and attacked from one more logical.

"But why punish me?" she protested. "Do *I* want the war? Do *I* want to free Cuba? No! I want *you*, and if you go, you are the one who is sure to be killed. You are so big—and so brave, and you will be rushing in wherever the fighting is, and then—then you will die." She raised her eyes and looked at him as though seeing him from a great distance. "And," she added fatefully, "I will die, too, or maybe I will have to live, to live without you for years, for many miserable years."

Fearfully, with great caution, as though in his joy in her he might crush her in his hands, the young man drew her to him and held her close. After a silence he whispered. "But, you know that nothing can happen to me. Not now, that

God has let me love you. He could not be so
cruel. He would not have given me such happiness to take it from me. A man who loves you,
as I love you, cannot come to any harm. And
the man *you* love is immortal, immune. He
holds a charmed life. So long as you love him,
he must live."

The eyes of the girl smiled up at him through
her tears. She lifted her lips to his. "Then
you will never die!" she said.

She held him away from her. "Listen!" she
whispered. "What you say is true. It must be
true, because you are always right. I love you
so that nothing can harm you. My love will
be a charm. It will hang around your neck
and protect you, and keep you, and bring you
back to me. When you are in danger my love
will save you. For, while it lives, I live. When
it dies——"

Chesterton kissed her quickly.

"What happens then," he said, "doesn't
matter."

The war game had run its happy-go-lucky
course briefly and brilliantly, with "glory enough
for all," even for Chesterton. For, in no
previous campaign had good fortune so per-
sistently stood smiling at his elbow. At each
moment of the war that was critical, picturesque,
dramatic, by some lucky accident he found him-

self among those present. He could not lose.
Even when his press boat broke down at Car-
denas, a Yankee cruiser and two Spanish gun-
boats, apparently for his sole benefit, engaged
in an impromptu duel within range of his megaphone. When his horse went lame, the column
with which he had wished to advance, passed
forward to the front unmolested, while the rear
guard, to which he had been forced to join his
fortune, fought its way through the stifling
underbrush.

Between his news despatches, when he was not
singing the praises of his fellow-countrymen, or
copying lists of their killed and wounded, he
wrote to Miss Armitage. His letters were
scrawled on yellow copy paper and consisted of
repetitions of the three words, "I love you,"
rearranged, illuminated, and intensified.

Each letter began much in the same way.
"The war is still going on. You can read about
it in the papers. What I want you to know is
that I love you as no man ever—" And so on
for many pages.

From her only one of the letters she wrote
reached him. It was picked up in the sand at
Siboney after the medical corps, in an effort to
wipe out the yellow-fever, had set fire to the
post-office tent.

She had written it some weeks before from

her summer home at Newport, and in it she said: "When you went to the front, I thought no woman could love more than I did then. But, now I know. At least I know one girl who can. She cannot write it. She can never tell you. You must just believe.

"Each day I hear from you, for as soon as the paper comes, I take it down to the rocks and read your cables, and I look south across the ocean to Cuba, and try to see you in all that fighting and heat and fever. But I am not afraid. For each morning I wake to find I love you more; that it has grown stronger, more wonderful, more hard to bear. And I know the charm I gave you grows with it, and is more powerful, and that it will bring you back to me wearing new honors, 'bearing your sheaves with you.'

"As though I cared for your new honors. I want *you, you, you*—only *you*."

When Santiago surrendered and the invading army settled down to arrange terms of peace, and imbibe fever, and General Miles moved to Porto Rico, Chesterton moved with him.

In that pretty little island a command of regulars under a general of the regular army had, in a night attack, driven back the Spaniards from Adhuntas. The next afternoon as the column was in line of march, and the men were shaking themselves into their accoutrements, a dusty, sweating volunteer staff officer rode down the main street of Adhuntas, and with the authority of a field marshal, held up his hand.

"General Miles's compliments, sir," he panted, "and peace is declared!"

Different men received the news each in a different fashion. Some whirled their hats in the air and cheered. Those who saw promotion and the new insignia on their straps vanish, swore deeply. Chesterton fell upon his saddle-bags and began to distribute his possessions among the enlisted men. After he had remobilized, his effects consisted of a change of clothes, his camera, water-bottle, and his medicine case. In his present state of health and spirits he could not believe he stood in need of the medicine case, but it was a gift from Miss Armitage, and carried with it a promise from him that he always would carry it. He had "packed" it throughout the campaign, and for others it had proved of value.

"I take it you are leaving us," said an officer enviously.

"I am leaving so quick," cried Chesterton laughing, "that you won't even see the dust. There's a transport starts from Mayaguez at six to-morrow morning, and, if I don't catch it, this pony will die on the wharf."

# A CHARMED LIFE

"The road to Mayaguez is not healthy for Americans," said the general in command. "I don't think I ought to let you go. The enemy does not know peace is on yet, and there are a lot of guerillas——"

Chesterton shook his head in pitying wonder.

"Not let me go!" he exclaimed. "Why, General, you haven't enough men in your command to stop me, and as for the Spaniards and guerillas—! I'm homesick," cried the young man. "I'm so damned homesick that I am liable to die of it before the transport gets me to Sandy Hook."

"If you are shot up by an outpost," growled the general, "you will be worse off than homesick. It's forty miles to Mayaguez. Better wait till daylight. Where's the sense of dying, after the fighting's over?"

"If I don't catch that transport I sure *will* die," laughed Chesterton. His head was bent and he was tugging at his saddle-girths. Apparently the effort brought a deeper shadow to his tan, "but nothing else can kill me! I have a charm, General," he exclaimed.

"We hadn't noticed it," said the general.

The staff officers, according to regulations, laughed.

"It's not that kind of a charm," said Chesterton. "Good-by, General."

# A CHARMED LIFE

The road was hardly more than a trail, but the moon made it as light as day, and cast across it black tracings of the swinging vines and creepers; while high in the air it turned the polished surface of the palms into glittering silver. As he plunged into the cool depths of the forest Chesterton threw up his arms and thanked God that he was moving toward her. The luck that had accompanied him throughout the campaign had held until the end. Had he been forced to wait for a transport, each hour would have meant a month of torment, an arid, wasted place in his life. As it was, with each eager stride of El Capitan, his little Porto Rican pony, he was brought closer to her. He was so happy that as he galloped through the dark shadows of the jungle or out into the brilliant moonlight he shouted aloud and sang; and again as he urged El Capitan to greater bursts of speed, he explained in joyous, breathless phrases why it was that he urged him on.

"For she is wonderful and most beautiful," he cried, "the most glorious girl in all the world! And, if I kept her waiting, even for a moment, El Capitan, I would be unworthy—and I might lose her! So you see we ride for a great prize!"

The Spanish column that, the night before, had been driven from Adhuntas, now in ignorance of peace, occupied both sides of the valley through which ran the road to Mayaguez, and in ambush by the road itself had placed an outpost of two men. One was a sharp-shooter of the picked corps of the Guardia Civil, and one a sergeant of the regiment that lay hidden in the heights. If the Americans advanced toward Mayaguez, these men were to wait until the head of the column drew abreast of them, when they were to fire. The report of their rifles would be the signal for those in the hill above to wipe out the memory of Adhuntas.

Chesterton had been riding at a gallop, but, as he reached the place where the men lay in ambush, he pulled El Capitan to a walk, and took advantage of his first breathing spell to light his pipe. He had already filled it, and was now fumbling in his pocket for his match-box. The match-box was of wood such as one can buy, filled to the brim with matches, for one penny. But it was a most precious possession. In the early days of his interest in Miss Armitage, as they were once setting forth upon a motor trip, she had handed it to him.

"Why," he asked.

"You always forget to bring any," she said simply, "and have to borrow some."

The other men in the car, knowing this to be a just reproof, laughed sardonically, and at the laugh the girl had looked up in surprise. Chesterton, seeing the look, understood that her act, trifling as it was, had been sincere, had been inspired simply by thought of his comfort. And he asked himself why young Miss Armitage should consider his comfort, and why the fact that she did consider it should make him so extremely happy. And he decided it must be because she loved him and he loved her.

Having arrived at that conclusion, he had asked her to marry him, and upon the match-box had marked the date and the hour. Since then she had given him many pretty presents, marked with her initials, marked with his crest, with strange cabalistic mottoes that meant nothing to any one save themselves. But the wooden match-box was still the most valued of his possessions.

As he rode into the valley the rays of the moon fell fully upon him, and exposed him to the outpost as pitilessly as though he had been held in the circle of a search-light.

The bronzed Mausers pushed cautiously through the screen of vines. There was a pause, and the rifle of the sergeant wavered. When he spoke his tone was one of disappointment.

"He is a scout, riding alone," he said.

"He is an officer," returned the sharp-shooter,

excitedly. "The others follow. We should fire now and give the signal."

"He is no officer, he is a scout," repeated the sergeant. "They have sent him ahead to study the trail and to seek us. He may be a league in advance. If we shoot *him*, we only warn the others."

Chesterton was within fifty yards. After an excited and anxious search he had found the match-box in the wrong pocket. The eyes of the sharp-shooter frowned along the barrel of his rifle. With his chin pressed against the stock he whispered swiftly from the corner of his lips, "He is an officer! I am aiming where the strap crosses his heart. You aim at his belt. We fire together."

The heat of the tropic night and the strenuous gallop had covered El Capitan with a lather of sweat. The reins upon his neck dripped with it. The gauntlets with which Chesterton held them were wet. As he raised the matchbox it slipped from his fingers and fell noiselessly in the trail. With an exclamation he dropped to the road and to his knees, and groping in the dust began an eager search.

The sergeant caught at the rifle of the sharpshooter, and pressed it down.

"Look!" he whispered. "He *is* a scout. He is searching the trail for the tracks of our ponies. If you fire they will hear it a league away."

"But if he finds our trail and returns——"

The sergeant shook his head. "I let him pass forward," he said grimly. "He will never return."

Chesterton pounced upon the half-buried match-box, and in a panic lest he might again lose it, thrust it inside his tunic.

"Little do you know, El Capitan," he exclaimed breathlessly, as he scrambled back into the saddle and lifted the pony into a gallop, "what a narrow escape I had. I almost lost it."

Toward midnight they came to a wooden bridge swinging above a ravine in which a mountain stream, forty feet below, splashed over half-hidden rocks, and the stepping stones of the ford. Even before the campaign began the bridge had outlived its usefulness, and the unwonted burden of artillery, and the vibrations of marching men had so shaken it that it swayed like a house of cards. Threatened by its own weight, at the mercy of the first tropic storm, it hung a death trap for the one who first added to its burden.

No sooner had El Capitan struck it squarely with his four hoofs, than he reared and, whirling, sprang back to the solid earth. The suddenness of his retreat had all but thrown Chesterton, but he regained his seat, and digging the pony roughly with his spurs, pulled his head again toward the bridge.

"What are you shying at, now?" he panted. "That's a perfectly good bridge."

For a minute horse and man struggled for the mastery, the horse spinning in short circles, the man pulling, tugging, urging him with knees and spurs. The first round ended in a draw. There were two more rounds with the advantage slightly in favor of El Capitan, for he did not approach the bridge.

The night was warm and the exertion violent. Chesterton, puzzled and annoyed, paused to regain his breath and his temper. Below him, in the ravine, the shallow waters of the ford called to him, suggesting a pleasant compromise. He turned his eyes downward and saw hanging over the water what appeared to be a white bird upon the lower limb of a dead tree. He knew it to be an orchid, an especially rare orchid, and he knew, also, that the orchid was the favorite flower of Miss Armitage. In a moment he was on his feet, and with the reins over his arm, was slipping down the bank, dragging El Capitan behind him. He ripped from the dead tree the bark to which the orchid was clinging, and with wet moss and grass packed it in his leather camera case. The camera he abandoned on the path.

He always could buy another camera; he could not again carry a white orchid, plucked in the heart of the tropics on the night peace was declared, to the girl he left behind him. Followed by El Capitan, nosing and snuffing gratefully at the cool waters, he waded the ford, and with his camera case swinging from his shoulder, galloped up the opposite bank and back into the trail.

A minute later, the bridge, unable to recover from the death blow struck by El Capitan, went whirling into the ravine and was broken upon the rocks below. Hearing the crash behind him, Chesterton guessed that in the jungle a tree had fallen.

They had started at six in the afternoon and had covered twenty of the forty miles that lay between Adhuntas and Mayaguez, when, just at the outskirts of the tiny village of Caguan, El Capitan stumbled, and when he arose painfully, he again fell forward.

Caguan was a little church, a little vine-covered inn, a dozen one-story adobe houses shining in the moonlight like whitewashed sepulchres. They faced a grass-grown plaza, in the centre of which stood a great wooden cross. At one corner of the village was a corral, and in it many ponies. At the sight Chesterton gave a cry of relief. A light showed through the

closed shutters of the inn, and when he beat
with his whip upon the door, from the adobe
houses other lights shone, and white-clad figures
appeared in the moonlight. The landlord of the
inn was a Spaniard, fat and prosperous-looking,
but for the moment his face was eloquent with
such distress and misery that the heart of the
young man, who was at peace with all the world,
went instantly out to him. The Spaniard was
less sympathetic. When he saw the khaki suit
and the campaign hat he scowled, and ungra-
ciously would have closed the door. Chesterton,
apologizing, pushed it open. His pony, he explained, had gone lame, and he must have
another, and at once. The landlord shrugged
his shoulders. These were war times, he said,
and the American officer could take what he
liked. They in Caguan were non-combatants
and could not protest. Chesterton hastened to
reassure him. The war, he announced, was
over, and were it not, he was no officer to issue
requisitions. He intended to pay for the pony.
He unbuckled his belt and poured upon the table
a handful of Spanish *doubloons*. The landlord
lowered the candle and silently counted the
gold pieces, and then calling to him two of his
fellow-villagers, crossed the tiny plaza and
entered the corral.

"The American pig," he whispered, "wishes to

buy a pony. He tells me the war is over; that
Spain has surrendered. We know that must be
a lie. It is more probable he is a deserter. He
claims he is a civilian, but that also is a lie, for
he is in uniform. You, Paul, sell him your
pony, and then wait for him at the first turn in
the trail, and take it from him."

"He is armed," protested the one called
Paul.

"You must not give him time to draw his
revolver," ordered the landlord. "You and
Pedro will shoot him from the shadow. He is
our country's enemy, and it will be in a good
cause. And he may carry despatches. If we
take them to the commandante at Mayaguez
he will reward us."

"And the gold pieces?" demanded the one
called Paul.

"We will divide them in three parts," said
the landlord.

In the front of the inn, surrounded by a ghost-
like group that spoke its suspicions, Chesterton
was lifting his saddle from El Capitan and rubbing the lame foreleg. It was not a serious
sprain. A week would set it right, but for that
night the pony was useless. Impatiently, Chesterton called across the plaza, begging the landlord to make haste. He was eager to be gone,
alarmed and fearful lest even this slight delay

should cause him to miss the transport. The thought was intolerable. But he was also acutely conscious that he was very hungry, and he was too old a campaigner to scoff at hunger. With the hope that he could find something to carry with him and eat as he rode forward, he entered the inn.

The main room of the house was now in darkness, but a smaller room adjoining it was lit by candles, and by a tiny taper floating before a crucifix. In the light of the candles Chesterton made out a bed, a priest bending over it, a woman kneeling beside it, and upon the bed the little figure of a boy tossed and moaned. As Chesterton halted and waited hesitating, the priest strode past him, and in a voice dull and flat with grief and weariness, ordered those at the door to bring the landlord quickly. As one of the group leaped toward the corral, the priest said to the others: "There is another attack. I have lost hope."

Chesterton advanced and asked if he could be of service. The priest shook his head. The child, he said, was the only son of the landlord, and much beloved by him, and by all the village. He was now in the third week of typhoid fever and the period of hemorrhages. Unless they could be checked, the boy would die, and the priest, who for many miles of mountain and forest was also the only doctor, had exhausted his store of simple medicines.

"Nothing can stop the hemorrhage," he protested wearily, "but the strongest of drugs. And I have nothing!"

Chesterton bethought him of the medicine case Miss Armitage had forced upon him. "I have given opium to the men for dysentery," he said. "Would opium help you?"

The priest sprang at him and pushed him out of the door and toward the saddle-bags.

"My children," he cried, to the silent group in the plaza, "God has sent a miracle!"

After an hour at the bedside the priest said, "He will live," and knelt, and the mother of the boy and the villagers knelt with him. When Chesterton raised his eyes, he found that the landlord, who had been silently watching while the two men struggled with death for the life of his son, had disappeared. But he heard, leaving the village along the trail to Mayaguez, the sudden clatter of a pony's hoofs. It moved like a thing driven with fear.

The priest strode out into the moonlight. In the recovery of the child he saw only a demonstration of the efficacy of prayer, and he could not too quickly bring home the lesson to his parishioners. Amid their murmurs of wonder and gratitude Chesterton rode away.

To the kindly care of the priest he bequeathed
El Capitan. With him, also, he left the gold
pieces which were to pay for the fresh pony.

A quarter of a mile outside the village three
white figures confronted him. Two who stood
apart in the shadow shrank from observation,
but the landlord, seated bareback upon a pony
that from some late exertion was breathing
heavily, called to him to halt.

"In the fashion of my country," he began
grandiloquently, "we have come this far to wish
you God speed upon your journey." In the
fashion of the American he seized Chesterton by
the hand. I thank you, señor," he murmured.

"Not me," returned Chesterton. "But the
one who made me 'pack' that medicine chest.
Thank her, for to-night, I think, it saved a life."

The Spaniard regarded him curiously, fixing
him with his eyes as though deep in consideration. At last he smiled gravely.

"You are right," he said. "Let us both
remember her in our prayers."

As Chesterton rode away the words remained
gratefully in his memory and filled him with
pleasant thoughts. "The world," he mused,
"is full of just such kind and gentle souls."

After an interminable delay he reached Newport, and they escaped from the others, and Miss

Armitage and he ran down the lawn to the rocks, and stood with the waves whispering at their feet.

It was the moment for which each had so often longed, with which both had so often tortured themselves by living in imagination, that now, that it was theirs, they were fearful it might not be true.

Finally, he said: "And the charm never failed! Indeed, it was wonderful! It stood by me so obviously. For instance, the night before San Juan, in the mill at El Poso, I slept on the same poncho with another correspondent. I woke up with a raging appetite for bacon and coffee, and he woke up out of his mind, and with a temperature of one hundred and four. And again, I was standing by Capron's gun at El Caney, when a shell took the three men who served it, and only scared *me*. And there was another time—" He stopped. "Anyway," he laughed, "here I am."

"But there was one night, one awful night," began the girl. She trembled, and he made this an added excuse for drawing her closer to him. "When I felt you were in great peril, that you would surely die. And all through the night I knelt by the window and looked toward Cuba and prayed, and prayed to God to let you live."

Chesterton bent his head and kissed the tips of her fingers. After a moment he said: "Would you know what night it was? It might be curious if I had been——"

"Would I know!" cried the girl. "It was eight days ago. The night of the twelfth. An awful night!"

"The twelfth!" exclaimed Chesterton, and laughed and then begged her pardon humbly. "I laughed because the twelfth," he exclaimed, "was the night peace was declared. The war was over. I'm sorry, but *that* night I was riding toward you, thinking only of you. I was never for a moment in danger."

# THE AMATEUR

## I

It was February, off the Banks, and so thick was the weather that, on the upper decks, one could have driven a sleigh. Inside the smoking-room Austin Ford, as securely sheltered from the blizzard as though he had been sitting in front of a wood fire at his club, ordered hot gin for himself and the ship's doctor. The ship's doctor had gone below on another "hurry call" from the widow. At the first luncheon on board the widow had sat on the right of Doctor Sparrow, with Austin Ford facing her. But since then, except to the doctor, she had been invisible. So, at frequent intervals, the ill health of the widow had deprived Ford of the society of the doctor. That it deprived him, also, of the society of the widow did not concern him. *Her* life had not been spent upon ocean liners; she could not remember when state-rooms were named after the States of the Union. She could not tell him of shipwrecks and salvage, of smugglers and of the modern pirates who found their victims in the smoking-room.

Ford was on his way to England to act as the London correspondent of the New York *Republic*. For three years on that most sensational of the New York dailies he had been the star man, the chief muckraker, the chief sleuth. His interest was in crime. Not in crimes committed in passion or inspired by drink, but in such offenses against law and society as are perpetrated with nice intelligence. The murderer, the burglar, the strong-arm men who, in side streets, waylay respectable citizens did not appeal to him. The man he studied, pursued, and exposed was the cashier who evolved a new method of covering up his peculations, the dishonest president of an insurance company, the confidence man who used no concealed weapon other than his wit. Toward the criminals he pursued young Ford felt no personal animosity. He harassed them as he would have shot a hawk killing chickens. Not because he disliked the hawk, but because the battle was unequal, and because he felt sorry for the chickens.

Had you called Austin Ford an amateur detective he would have been greatly annoyed. He argued that his position was similar to that of the dramatic critic. The dramatic critic warned the public against bad plays; Ford warned it against bad men. Having done that, he left it to the public to determine whether the bad man should thrive or perish.

When the managing editor told him of his appointment to London, Ford had protested that his work lay in New York; that of London and the English, except as a tourist and sightseer, he knew nothing.

"That's just why we are sending you," explained the managing editor. "Our readers are ignorant. To make them read about London you've got to tell them about themselves in London. They like to know who's been presented at court, about the American girls who have married dukes; and which ones opened a bazaar, and which one opened a hat shop, and which is getting a divorce. Don't send us anything concerning suffragettes and Dreadnaughts. Just send us stuff about Americans. If you take your meals in the Carlton grill-room and drink at the Cecil you can pick up more good stories than we can print. You will find lots of your friends over there. Some of those girls who married dukes," he suggested, "know you, don't they?"

"Not since they married dukes," said Ford.

"Well, anyway, all your other friends will be there," continued the managing editor encouragingly. "Now that they have shut up the tracks here all the con men have gone to London. They say an American can't take a drink at the Salisbury without his fellow-countrymen having a fight as to which one will sell him a gold brick."

Ford's eyes lightened in pleasurable anticipation.

"Look them over," urged the managing editor, "and send us a special. Call it 'The American Invasion.' Don't you see a story in it?"

"It will be the first one I send you," said Ford.

The ship's doctor returned from his visit below decks and sank into the leather cushion close to Ford's elbow. For a few moments the older man sipped doubtfully at his gin and water, and, as though perplexed, rubbed his hand over his bald and shining head. "I told her to talk to you," he said fretfully.

"Her? Who?" inquired Ford. "Oh, the widow?"

"You were right about that," said Doctor Sparrow; "she is not a widow."

The reporter smiled complacently.

"Do you know why I thought not?" he demanded. "Because all the time she was at luncheon she kept turning over her weddingring as though she was not used to it. It was a new ring, too. I told you then she was not a widow."

"Do you always notice things like that?" asked the doctor.

"Not on purpose," said the amateur detective; "I can't help it. I see ten things where other people see only one; just as some men run ten times as fast as other men. We have tried it out often at the office; put all sorts of junk under a newspaper, lifted the newspaper for five seconds, and then each man wrote down what he had seen. Out of twenty things I would remember seventeen. The next best guess would be about nine. Once I saw a man lift his coat collar to hide his face. It was in the Grand Central Station. I stopped him, and told him he was wanted. Turned out he *was* wanted. It was Goldberg, making his getaway to Canada."

"It is a gift," said the doctor.

"No, it's a nuisance," laughed the reporter. "I see so many things I don't want to see. I see that people are wearing clothes that are not made for them. I see when women are lying to me. I can see when men are on the verge of a nervous breakdown, and whether it is drink or debt or morphine——"

The doctor snorted triumphantly.

"You did not see that the widow was on the verge of a breakdown!"

"No," returned the reporter. "Is she? I'm sorry."

"If you're sorry," urged the doctor eagerly, "you'll help her. She is going to London alone to find her husband. He has disappeared. She thinks that he has been murdered, or that he is lying ill in some hospital. I told her if any one could help her to find him you could. I had to say something. She's very ill."

"To find her husband in London?" repeated Ford. "London is a large town."

"She has photographs of him and she knows where he spends his time," pleaded the doctor. "He is a company promoter. It should be easy for you."

"Maybe he doesn't want her to find him," said Ford. "Then it wouldn't be so easy for me."

The old doctor sighed heavily. "I know," he murmured. "I thought of that, too. And she is so very pretty."

"That was another thing I noticed," said Ford. The doctor gave no heed.

"She must stop worrying," he exclaimed, "or she will have a mental collapse. I have tried sedatives, but they don't touch her. I want to give her courage. She is frightened. She's left a baby boy at home, and she's fearful that something will happen to him, and she's frightened at being at sea, frightened at being alone in London; it's pitiful." The old man shook

his head. "Pitiful! Will you talk to her now?"
he asked.

"Nonsense!" exclaimed Ford. "She doesn't
want to tell the story of her life to strange
young men."

"But it was she suggested it," cried the
doctor. "She asked me if you were Austin
Ford, the great detective."

Ford snorted scornfully. "She did not!" he
protested. His tone was that of a man who
hopes to be contradicted.

"But she did," insisted the doctor, "and I
told her your specialty was tracing persons.
Her face lightened at once; it gave her hope.
She will listen to you. Speak very gently and
kindly and confidently. Say you are sure you
can find him."

"Where is the lady now?" asked Ford.

Doctor Sparrow scrambled eagerly to his feet.
"She cannot leave her cabin," he answered.

The widow, as Ford and Doctor Sparrow still
thought of her, was lying on the sofa that ran
the length of the stateroom, parallel with the
lower berth. She was fully dressed, except that
instead of her bodice she wore a kimono that
left her throat and arms bare. She had been
sleeping, and when their entrance awoke her,
her blue eyes regarded them uncomprehendingly.
Ford, hidden from her by the doctor, observed

that not only was she very pretty, but that she was absurdly young, and that the drowsy smile she turned upon the old man before she noted the presence of Ford was as innocent as that of a baby. Her cheeks were flushed, her eyes brilliant, her yellow curls had become loosened and were spread upon the pillow. When she saw Ford she caught the kimono so closely around her throat that she choked. Had the doctor not pushed her down she would have stood.

"I thought," she stammered, "he was an *old* man."

The doctor, misunderstanding, hastened to reassure her. "Mr. Ford is old in experience," he said soothingly. "He has had remarkable success. Why, he found a criminal once just because the man wore a collar. And he found Walsh, the burglar, and Phillips, the forger, and a gang of counterfeiters——"

Mrs. Ashton turned upon him, her eyes wide with wonder. "But *my* husband," she protested, "is not a criminal!"

"My dear lady!" the doctor cried. "I did not mean that, of course not. I meant, if Mr. Ford can find men who don't wish to be found, how easy for him to find a man who——" He turned helplessly to Ford. "You tell her," he begged.

Ford sat down on a steamer-trunk that protruded from beneath the berth, and, turning to the widow, gave her the full benefit of his working smile. It was confiding, helpless, appealing. It showed a trustfulness in the person to whom it was addressed that caused that individual to believe Ford needed protection from a wicked world.

"Doctor Sparrow tells me," began Ford timidly, "you have lost your husband's address; that you will let me try to find him. If I can help in any way I should be glad."

The young girl regarded him, apparently, with disappointment. It was as though Doctor Sparrow had led her to expect a man full of years and authority, a man upon whom she could lean; not a youth whose smile seemed to beg one not to scold him. She gave Ford three photographs, bound together with a string.

"When Doctor Sparrow told me you could help me I got out these," she said.

Ford jotted down a mental note to the effect that she "got them out." That is, she did not keep them where she could always look at them. That she was not used to look at them was evident by the fact that they were bound together.

The first photograph showed three men standing in an open place and leaning on a railing.

One of them was smiling toward the photographer. He was a good-looking young man of about thirty years of age, well fed, well dressed, and apparently well satisfied with the world and himself. Ford's own smile had disappeared. His eyes were alert and interested.

"The one with the Panama hat pulled down over his eyes is your husband?" he asked.

"Yes," assented the widow. Her tone showed slight surprise.

"This was taken about a year ago?" inquired Ford. "Must have been," he answered himself; "they haven't raced at the Bay since then. This was taken in front of the club stand— probably for the *Telegraph?*" He lifted his eyes inquiringly.

Rising on her elbow the young wife bent forward toward the photograph. "Does it say that there?" she asked doubtfully. "How did you guess that?"

In his rôle as chorus the ship's doctor exclaimed with enthusiasm: "Didn't I tell you? He's wonderful."

Ford cut him off impatiently. "You never saw a rail as high as that except around a racetrack," he muttered. "And the badge in his buttonhole and the angle of the stand all show——"

He interrupted himself to address the widow.

"This is an owner's badge. What was the name of his stable?"

"I don't know," she answered. She regarded the young man with sudden uneasiness. "They only owned one horse, but I believe that gave them the privilege of——"

"I see," exclaimed Ford. "Your husband is a bookmaker. But in London he is a promoter of companies."

"So my friend tells me," said Mrs. Ashton. "She's just got back from London. Her husband told her that Harry, my husband, was always at the American bar in the Cecil or at the Salisbury or the Savoy." The girl shook her head. "But a woman can't go looking for a man there," she protested. "That's, why I thought you——"

"That'll be all right," Ford assured her hurriedly. "It's a coincidence, but it happens that my own work takes me to these hotels, and if your husband is there I will find him." He returned the photographs.

"Hadn't you better keep one?" she asked.

"I won't forget him," said the reporter. "Besides"—he turned his eyes toward the doctor and, as though thinking aloud, said—"he may have grown a beard."

There was a pause.

The eyes of the woman grew troubled. Her

lips pressed together as though in a sudden access of pain.

"And he may," Ford continued, "have changed his name."

As though fearful, if she spoke, the tears would fall, the girl nodded her head stiffly.

Having learned what he wanted to know Ford applied to the wound a soothing ointment of promises and encouragement.

"He's as good as found," he protested. "You will see him in a day, two days after you land."

The girl's eyes opened happily. She clasped her hands together and raised them.

"You will try?" she begged. "You will find him for me"—she corrected herself eagerly— "for me and the baby?"

The loose sleeves of the kimono fell back to her shoulders showing the white arms; the eyes raised to Ford were glistening with tears.

"Of course I will find him," growled the reporter.

He freed himself from the appeal in the eyes of the young mother and left the cabin. The doctor followed. He was bubbling over with enthusiasm.

"That was fine!" he cried. "You said just the right thing. There will be no collapse now."

His satisfaction was swept away in a burst of disgust.

"The blackguard!" he protested. "To desert a wife as young as that and as pretty as that."

"So I have been thinking," said the reporter. "I guess," he added gravely, "what is going to happen is that before I find her husband I will have got to know him pretty well."

Apparently, young Mrs. Ashton believed everything would come to pass just as Ford promised it would and as he chose to order it; for the next day, with a color not born of fever in her cheeks and courage in her eyes, she joined Ford and the doctor at the luncheon-table. Her attention was concentrated on the younger man. In him she saw the one person who could bring her husband to her.

"She acts," growled the doctor later in the smoking-room, "as though she was afraid you were going to back out of your promise and jump overboard.

"Don't think," he protested violently, "it's you she's interested in. All she sees in you is what you can do for her. Can you see that?"

"Any one as clever at seeing things as I am," returned the reporter, "cannot help but see that."

Later, as Ford was walking on the upper deck, Mrs. Ashton came toward him, beating her way against the wind. Without a trace of coquetry or self-consciousness, and with a sigh of content, she laid her hand on his arm.

"When I don't see you," she exclaimed as simply as a child, "I feel so frightened. When I see you I know all will come right. Do you mind if I walk with you?" she asked. "And do you mind if every now and then I ask you to tell me again it will all come right?"

For the three days following Mrs. Ashton and Ford were constantly together. Or, at least, Mrs. Ashton was constantly with Ford. She told him that when she sat in her cabin the old fears returned to her, and in these moments of panic she searched the ship for him.

The doctor protested that he was growing jealous.

"I'm not so greatly to be envied," suggested Ford. " 'Harry' at meals three times a day and on deck all the rest of the day becomes monotonous. On a closer acquaintance with Harry he seems to be a decent sort of a young man; at least he seems to have been at one time very much in love with her."

"Well," sighed the doctor sentimentally, "she is certainly very much in love with Harry."

Ford shook his head non-committingly. "I don't know her story," he said. "Don't want to know it."

The ship was in the Channel, on her way to

Cherbourg, and running as smoothly as a clock.
From the shore friendly lights told them they
were nearing their journey's end; that the land
was on every side. Seated on a steamer-chair
next to his in the semi-darkness of the deck,
Mrs. Ashton began to talk nervously and
eagerly.

"Now that we are so near," she murmured,
"I have got to tell you something. If you did
not know I would feel I had not been fair. You
might think that when you were doing so much
for me I should have been more honest."

She drew a long breath. "It's so hard," she
said.

"Wait," commanded Ford. "Is it going to
help me to find him?"

"No."

"Then don't tell me."

His tone caused the girl to start. She leaned
toward him and peered into his face. His eyes,
as he looked back to her, were kind and com-
prehending.

"You mean," said the amateur detective,
"that your husband has deserted you. That if
it were not for the baby you would not try to
find him. Is that it?"

Mrs. Ashton breathed quickly and turned her
face away.

"Yes," she whispered. "That is it."

There was a long pause. When she faced him again the fact that there was no longer a secret between them seemed to give her courage.

"Maybe," she said, "you can understand. Maybe you can tell me what it means. I have thought and thought. I have gone over it and over it until when I go back to it my head aches. I have done nothing else but think, and I can't make it seem better. I can't find any excuse. I have had no one to talk to, no one I could tell. I have thought maybe a man could understand." She raised her eyes appealingly.

"If you can only make it seem less cruel. Don't you see," she cried miserably, "I want to believe; I want to forgive him. I want to think he loves me. Oh! I want so to be able to love him; but how can I? I can't! I can't!"

In the week in which they had been thrown together the girl unconsciously had told Ford much about herself and her husband. What she now told him was but an amplification of what he had guessed.

She had met Ashton a year and a half before, when she had just left school at the convent and had returned to live with her family. Her home was at Far Rockaway. Her father was a cashier in a bank at Long Island City. One night, with a party of friends, she had been taken to a dance at one of the beach hotels, and there met Ashton. At that time he was one of a firm that was making book at the Aqueduct race-track. The girl had met very few men and with them was shy and frightened, but with Ashton she found herself at once at ease. That night he drove her and her friends home in his touring-car and the next day they teased her about her conquest. It made her very happy. After that she went to hops at the hotel, and as the bookmaker did not dance, the two young people sat upon the piazza. Then Ashton came to see her at her own house, but when her father learned that the young man who had been calling upon her was a bookmaker he told him he could not associate with his daughter.

But the girl was now deeply in love with Ashton, and apparently he with her. He begged her to marry him. They knew that to this, partly from prejudice and partly owing to his position in the bank, her father would object. Accordingly they agreed that in August, when the racing moved to Saratoga, they would run away and get married at that place. Their plan was that Ashton would leave for Saratoga with the other racing men, and that she would join him the next day.

They had arranged to be married by a magistrate, and Ashton had shown her a letter from one at Saratoga who consented to perform the ceremony. He had given her an engagement ring and two thousand dollars, which he asked her to keep for him, lest tempted at the track he should lose it.

But she assured Ford it was not such material things as a letter, a ring, or gift of money that had led her to trust Ashton. His fear of losing her, his complete subjection to her wishes, his happiness in her presence, all seemed to prove that to make her happy was his one wish, and that he could do anything to make her unhappy appeared impossible.

They were married the morning she arrived at Saratoga; and the same day departed for Niagara Falls and Quebec. The honeymoon lasted ten days. They were ten days of complete happiness. No one, so the girl declared, could have been more kind, more unselfishly considerate than her husband. They returned to Saratoga and engaged a suite of rooms at one of the big hotels. Ashton was not satisfied with the rooms shown him, and leaving her upstairs returned to the office floor to ask for others.

Since that moment his wife had never seen him nor heard from him.

On the day of her marriage young Mrs. Ashton had written to her father, asking him to give her his good wishes and pardon. He refused both.

As she had feared, he did not consider that for a bank clerk a gambler made a desirable son-in-law; and the letters he wrote his daughter were so bitter that in reply she informed him he had forced her to choose between her family and her husband, and that she chose her husband. In consequence, when she found herself deserted she felt she could not return to her people. She remained in Saratoga. There she moved into cheap lodgings, and in order that the two thousand dollars Ashton had left with her might be saved for his child, she had learned to typewrite, and after four months had been able to support herself. Within the last month a girl friend, who had known both Ashton and herself before they were married, had written her that her husband was living in London. For the sake of her son she had at once determined to make an effort to seek him out.

"The son, nonsense!" exclaimed the doctor, when Ford retold the story. "She is not crossing the ocean because she is worried about the future of her son. She seeks her own happiness. The woman is in love with her husband."

Ford shook his head.

"I don't know!" he objected. "She's so extravagant in her praise of Harry that it seems unreal. It sounds insincere. Then, again, when I swear I will find him she shows a delight that you might describe as savage, almost vindictive. As though, if I did find Harry, the first thing she would do would be to stick a knife in him."

"Maybe," volunteered the doctor sadly, "she has heard there is a woman in the case. Maybe she is the one she's thinking of sticking the knife into?"

"Well," declared the reporter, "if she doesn't stop looking savage every time I promise to find Harry I won't find Harry. Why should I act the part of Fate, anyway? How do I know that Harry hasn't got a wife in London and several in the States? How do we know he didn't leave his country for his country's good? That's what it looks like to me. How can we tell what confronted him the day he went down to the hotel desk to change his rooms and, instead, got into his touring-car and beat the speed limit to Canada? Whom did he meet in the hotel corridor? A woman with a perfectly good marriage certificate, or a detective with a perfectly good warrant? Or did Harry find out that his bride had a devil of a temper of her own, and that for him marriage was a failure? The widow is certainly a very charming young woman, but there may be two sides to this."

"You are a cynic, sir," protested the doctor.

"That may be," growled the reporter, "but I am not a private detective agency, or a matrimonial bureau, and before I hear myself saying, 'Bless you, my children!' both of these young people will have to show me why they should not be kept asunder."

## II

On the afternoon of their arrival in London Ford convoyed Mrs. Ashton to an old-established private hotel in Craven Street.

"Here," he explained, "you will be within a few hundred yards of the place in which your husband is said to spend his time. I will be living in the same hotel. If I find him you will know it in ten minutes."

The widow gave a little gasp, whether of excitement or of happiness Ford could not determine.

"Whatever happens," she begged, "will you let me hear from you sometimes? You are the only person I know in London—and—it's so big it frightens me. I don't want to be a burden," she went on eagerly, "but if I can feel you are within call——"

"What you need," said Ford heartily, "is less of the doctor's nerve tonic and sleeping drafts, and a little innocent diversion. To-night I am going to take you to the Savoy to supper."

Mrs. Ashton exclaimed delightedly, and then was filled with misgivings.

"I have nothing to wear," she protested, "and over here, in the evening, the women dress so well. I have a dinner gown," she exclaimed, "but it's black. Would that do?"

Ford assured her nothing could be better. He had a man's vanity in liking a woman with whom he was seen in public to be pretty and smartly dressed, and he felt sure that in black the blond beauty of Mrs. Ashton would appear to advantage. They arranged to meet at eleven on the promenade leading to the Savoy supper-room, and parted with mutual satisfaction at the prospect.

The finding of Harry Ashton was so simple that in its very simplicity it appeared spectacular.

On leaving Mrs. Ashton, Ford engaged rooms at the Hotel Cecil. Before visiting his rooms he made his way to the American bar. He did not go there seeking Harry Ashton. His object was entirely self-centred. His purpose was to drink to himself and to the lights of London. But as though by appointment, the man he had promised to find was waiting for him. As Ford entered the room, at a table facing the door sat Ashton. There was no mistaking him.

He wore a mustache, but it was disguise. He was the same good-natured, good-looking youth who, in the photograph from under a Panama hat, had smiled upon the world. With a glad cry Ford rushed toward him.

"Fancy meeting *you!*" he exclaimed.

Mr. Ashton's good-natured smile did not relax. He merely shook his head.

"Afraid you have made a mistake," he said.

The reporter regarded him blankly. His face showed his disappointment.

"Aren't you Charles W. Garrett, of New York?" he demanded.

"Not me," said Mr. Ashton.

"But," Ford insisted in hurt tones, as though he were being trifled with, "you have been told you look like him, haven't you?"

Mr. Ashton's good nature was unassailable.

"Sorry," he declared, "never heard of him."

Ford became garrulous, he could not believe two men could look so much alike. It was a remarkable coincidence. The stranger must certainly have a drink, the drink intended for his twin. Ashton was bored, but accepted. He was well acquainted with the easy good-fellowship of his countrymen. The room in which he sat was a meeting-place for them. He considered that they were always giving each other drinks, and not only were they always introducing themselves, but saying, "Shake hands with my friend, Mr. So-and-So." After five minutes they showed each other photographs of the children. This one, though as loquacious as the others, seemed better dressed, more "wise"; he brought to the exile the atmosphere of his beloved Broadway, so Ashton drank to him pleasantly.

"My name is Sydney Carter," he volunteered.

As a poker-player skims over the cards in his hand, Ford, in his mind's eye, ran over the value of giving or not giving his right name. He decided that Ashton would not have heard it and that, if he gave a false one, there was a chance that later Ashton might find out that he had done so. Accordingly he said, "Mine is Austin Ford," and seated himself at Ashton's table. Within ten minutes the man he had promised to pluck from among the eight million inhabitants of London was smiling sympathetically at his jests and buying a drink.

On the steamer Ford had rehearsed the story with which, should he meet Ashton, he would introduce himself. It was one arranged to fit with his theory that Ashton was a crook. If Ashton were a crook Ford argued that to at once ingratiate himself in his good graces he also must be a crook. His plan was to invite Ashton to co-operate with him in some scheme that was openly dishonest. By so doing he hoped apparently to place himself at Ashton's mercy. He believed if he could persuade Ashton he was more of a rascal than Ashton himself, and an exceedingly stupid rascal, any distrust the bookmaker might feel toward him would disappear. He made his advances so openly, and apparently showed his hand so carelessly, that, from being bored, Ashton became puzzled, then interested; and when Ford insisted he should dine with him, he considered it so necessary to find out who the youth might be who was forcing himself upon him that he accepted the invitation.

They adjourned to dress and an hour later, at Ford's suggestion, they met at the Carlton. There Ford ordered a dinner calculated to lull his newly made friend into a mood suited to confidence, but which had on Ashton exactly the opposite effect. Merely for the pleasure of his company, utter strangers were not in the habit of treating him to strawberries in February, and vintage champagne; and, in consequence, in Ford's hospitality he saw only cause for suspicion. If, as he had first feared, Ford was a New York detective, it was most important he should know that. No one better than Ashton understood that, at that moment, his presence in New York meant, for the police, unalloyed satisfaction, and for himself undisturbed solitude. But Ford was unlike any detective of his acquaintance; and his acquaintance had been extensive. It was true Ford was familiar with all the habits of Broadway and the Tenderloin. Of places with which Ashton was intimate, and of men with whom Ashton had formerly been well acquainted, he talked glibly. But, if he were a detective, Ashton considered, they certainly had improved the class.

The restaurant into which for the first time Ashton had penetrated, and in which he felt ill at ease, was to Ford, he observed, a matter of course. Evidently for Ford it held no terrors. He criticised the service, patronized the head waiters, and grumbled at the food; and when, on leaving the restaurant, an Englishman and his wife stopped at their table to greet him, he accepted their welcome to London without embarrassment.

Ashton, rolling his cigar between his lips, observed the incident with increasing bewilderment.

"You've got some swell friends," he growled. "I'll bet you never met *them* at Healey's!"

"I meet all kinds of people in my business," said Ford. "I once sold that man some mining stock, and the joke of it was," he added, smiling knowingly, "it turned out to be good."

Ashton decided that the psychological moment had arrived.

"What *is* your business?" he asked.

"I'm a company promoter," said Ford easily. "I thought I told you."

"I did not tell you that I was a company promoter, too, did I?" demanded Ashton.

"No," answered Ford, with apparent surprise. "Are you? That's funny."

Ashton watched for the next move, but the subject seemed in no way to interest Ford. Instead of following it up he began afresh.

"Have you any money lying idle?" he asked abruptly. "About a thousand pounds."

Ashton recognized that the mysterious stranger was about to disclose both himself and whatever object he had in seeking him out. He cast a quick glance about him.

"I can always find money," he said guardedly. "What's the proposition?"

With pretended nervousness Ford leaned forward and began the story he had rehearsed. It was a new version of an old swindle and to every self-respecting confidence man was well known as the "sick engineer" game. The plot is very simple. The sick engineer is supposed to be a mining engineer who, as an expert, has examined a gold mine and reported against it. For his services the company paid him partly in stock.

He falls ill and is at the point of death. While he has been ill much gold has been found in the mine he examined, and the stock which he considers worthless is now valuable. Of this, owing to his illness, he is ignorant. One confidence man acts the part of the sick engineer, and the other that of a broker who knows the engineer possesses the stock but has no money with which to purchase it from him. For a share of the stock he offers to tell the dupe where it and the engineer can be found. They visit the man, apparently at the point of death, and the dupe gives him money for his stock. Later the dupe finds the stock is worthless, and the supposed engineer and the supposed broker divide the money he paid for it. In telling the story Ford pretended he was the broker and that he thought in Ashton he had found a dupe who would buy the stock from the sick engineer.

As the story unfolded and Ashton appreciated the part Ford expected him to play in it, his emotions were so varied that he was in danger of apoplexy. Amusement, joy, chagrin, and indignation illuminated his countenance. His cigar ceased to burn, and with his eyes opened wide he regarded Ford in pitying wonder.

"Wait!" he commanded. He shook his head uncomprehendingly. "Tell me," he asked, "do

"Do I look as easy as that, or are you just naturally foolish?"

I look as easy as that, or are you just naturally foolish?"

Ford pretended to fall into a state of great alarm.

"I don't understand," he stammered.

"Why, son," exclaimed Ashton kindly, "I was taught that story in the public schools. I invented it. I stopped using it before you cut your teeth. Gee!" he exclaimed delightedly. "I knew I had grown respectable-looking, but I didn't think I was so damned respectable-looking as that!" He began to laugh silently; so greatly was he amused that the tears shone in his eyes and his shoulders shook.

"I'm sorry for you, son," he protested, "but that's the funniest thing that's come my way in two years. And you buying me hot-house grapes, too, and fancy water! I wish you could see your face," he taunted.

Ford pretended to be greatly chagrined.

"All right," he declared roughly. "The laugh's on me this time, but just because I lost one trick, don't think I don't know my business. Now that I'm wise to what *you* are we can work together and——"

The face of young Mr. Ashton became instantly grave. His jaws snapped like a trap. When he spoke his tone was assured and slightly contemptuous.

THE AMATEUR

"Not with *me* you can't work!" he said.

"Don't think because I fell down on this," Ford began hotly.

"I'm not thinking of you at all," said Ashton. "You're a nice little fellow all right, but you have sized me up wrong. I am on the 'straight and narrow' that leads back to little old New York and God's country, and I am warranted not to run off my trolley."

The words were in the vernacular, but the tone in which the young man spoke rang so confidently that it brought to Ford a pleasant thrill of satisfaction. From the first he had found in the personality of the young man something winning and likable; a shrewd manliness and tolerant good-humor. His eyes may have shown his sympathy, for, in sudden confidence, Ashton leaned nearer.

"It's like this," he said. "Several years ago I made a bad break and, about a year later, they got onto me and I had to cut and run. In a month the law of limitation lets me loose and I can go back. And you can bet I'm *going* back. I will be on the bowsprit of the first boat. I've had all I want of the 'fugitive-from-justice' game, thank you, and I have taken good care to keep a clean bill of health so that I won't have to play it again. They've been trying to **get me** for several years—especially the Pinker-

218

tons. They have chased me all over Europe. Chased me with all kinds of men; sometimes with women; they've tried everything except blood-hounds. At first I thought *you* were a 'Pink,' that's why——"

"I!" interrupted Ford, exploding derisively. "That's *good*! That's one on *you*." He ceased laughing and regarded Ashton kindly. "How do you know I'm not?" he asked.

For an instant the face of the bookmaker grew a shade less red and his eyes searched those of Ford in a quick agony of suspicion. Ford continued to smile steadily at him, and Ashton breathed with relief.

"I'll take a chance with you," he said, "and if you are as bad a detective as you are a sport I needn't worry."

They both laughed, and, with sudden mutual liking, each raised his glass and nodded.

"But they haven't got me yet," continued Ashton, "and unless they get me in the next thirty days I'm free. So you needn't think that I'll help you. It's 'never again' for me. The first time, that was the fault of the crowd I ran with; the second time, that would be *my* fault. And there ain't going to be any second time."

He shook his head doggedly, and with squared shoulders leaned back in his chair.

"If it only breaks right for me," he declared, "I'll settle down in one of those 'Own-your-own-homes,' forty-five minutes from Broadway, and never leave the wife and the baby."

The words almost brought Ford to his feet. He had forgotten the wife and the baby. He endeavored to explain his surprise by a sudden assumption of incredulity.

"Fancy you married!" he exclaimed.

"Married!" protested Ashton. "I'm married to the finest little lady that ever wore skirts, and in thirty-seven days I'll see her again. Thirty-seven days," he repeated impatiently. "Gee! That's a hell of a long time!"

Ford studied the young man with increased interest. That he was speaking sincerely, from the heart, there seemed no possible doubt.

Ashton frowned and his face clouded. "I've not been able to treat her just right," he volunteered. "If she wrote me, the letters might give them a clew, and I don't write *her* because I don't want her to know all my troubles until they're over. But I know," he added, "that five minutes' talk will set it all right. That is, if she still feels about me the way I feel about her."

The man crushed his cigar in his fingers and threw the pieces on the floor. "That's what's been the worst!" he exclaimed bitterly. "Not hearing, not knowing. It's been hell!"

His eyes as he raised them were filled with suffering, deep and genuine.

Ford rose suddenly. "Let's go down to the Savoy for supper," he said.

"Supper!" growled Ashton. "What's the use of supper? Do you suppose cold chicken and a sardine can keep me from *thinking?*"

Ford placed his hand on the other's shoulder.

"You come with me," he said kindly. "I'm going to do you a favor. I'm going to bring you a piece of luck. Don't ask me any questions," he commanded hurriedly. "Just take my word for it."

They had sat so late over their cigars that when they reached the restaurant on the Embankment the supper-room was already partly filled, and the corridors and lounge were brilliantly lit and gay with well-dressed women. Ashton regarded the scene with gloomy eyes. Since he had spoken of his wife he had remained silent, chewing savagely on a fresh cigar. But Ford was grandly excited. He did not know exactly what he intended to do. He was prepared to let events direct themselves, but of two things he was assured: Mrs. Ashton loved her husband, and her husband loved her. As the god in the car who was to bring them together, he felt a delightful responsibility.

The young men left the coat-room and came down the short flight of steps that leads to the wide lounge of the restaurant. Ford slightly in advance, searching with his eyes for Mrs. Ashton, found her seated alone in the lounge, evidently waiting for him. At the first glance she was hardly to be recognized. Her low-cut dinner gown of black satin that clung to her like a wet bath robe was the last word of the new fashion; and since Ford had seen her her blond hair had been arranged by an artist. Her appearance was smart, elegant, daring. She was easily the prettiest and most striking-looking woman in the room, and for an instant Ford stood gazing at her, trying to find in the self-possessed young woman the deserted wife of the steamer. She did not see Ford. Her eyes were following the progress down the hall of a woman, and her profile was toward him.

The thought of the happiness he was about to bring to two young people gave Ford the sense of a genuine triumph, and when he turned to Ashton to point out his wife to him he was thrilling with pride and satisfaction. His triumph received a bewildering shock. Already Ashton had discovered the presence of Mrs. Ashton. He was standing transfixed, lost to his surroundings, devouring her with his eyes. And then, to the amazement of Ford, his eyes filled with fear, doubt, and anger. Swiftly, with the movement of a man ducking a blow, he turned and sprang up the stairs and into the coat-room. Ford, bewildered and more conscious of his surroundings, followed him less quickly, and was in consequence only in time to see Ashton, dragging his overcoat behind him, disappear into the court-yard. He seized his own coat and raced in pursuit. As he ran into the court-yard Ashton, in the Strand, was just closing the door of a taxicab, but before the chauffeur could free it from the surrounding traffic, Ford had dragged the door open, and leaped inside. Ashton was huddled in the corner, panting, his face pale with alarm.

"What the devil ails you?" roared Ford. "Are you trying to shake me? You've got to come back. You must speak to her."

"Speak to her!" repeated Ashton. His voice was sunk to a whisper. The look of alarm in his face was confused with one grim and menacing. "Did you know she was there?" he demanded softly. "Did you take me there, knowing——?"

"Of course I knew," protested Ford. "She's been looking for you——"

His voice subsided in a squeak of amazement and pain. Ashton's left hand had shot out and swiftly seized his throat. With the other he pressed an automatic revolver against Ford's shirt front.

"I know she's been looking for me," the man whispered thickly. "For two years she's been looking for me. I know all about *her!* But, *who in hell are you?*"

Ford, gasping and gurgling, protested loyally. "You are wrong!" he cried. "She's been at home waiting for you. She thinks you have deserted her and your baby. I tell you she loves you, you fool, she *loves* you!"

The fingers on his throat suddenly relaxed; the flaming eyes of Ashton, glaring into his, wavered and grew wide with amazement.

"Loves me," he whispered. "*Who* loves me?"

"Your wife," protested Ford; "the girl at the Savoy, your wife."

Again the fingers of Ashton pressed deep around his neck.

"That is not my wife," he whispered. His voice was unpleasantly cold and grim. "That's 'Baby Belle,' with her hair dyed, a detective lady of the Pinkertons, hired to find me. And *you* know it. Now, who are *you?*"

To permit him to reply Ashton released his hand, but at the same moment, in a sudden access of fear, dug the revolver deeper into the pit of Ford's stomach.

"Quick!" he commanded. "Never mind the girl. *Who are you?*"

# THE AMATEUR

Ford collapsed against the cushioned corner of the cab. "And she begged me to find you," he roared, "because she *loved* you, because she wanted to *believe* in you!" He held his arms above his head. "Go ahead and shoot!" he cried. "You want to know who I am?" he demanded. His voice rang with rage. "I'm an amateur. Just a natural-born fool-amateur! Go on and shoot!"

The gun in Ashton's hand sank to his knee. Between doubt and laughter his face was twisted in strange lines. The cab was whirling through a narrow, unlit street leading to Covent Garden. Opening the door Ashton called to the chauffeur, and then turned to Ford.

"You get off here!" he commanded. "Maybe you're a 'Pink,' maybe you're a good fellow. I think you're a good fellow, but I'm not taking any chances. Get out!"

Ford scrambled to the street, and as the taxi-cab again butted itself forward, Ashton leaned far through the window. "Good-by, son," he called. "Send me a picture-postal card to Paris. For I am off to Maxim's," he cried, "and you can go to——"

"Not at all!" shouted the amateur detective indignantly. "I'm going back to take supper with 'Baby Belle'!"

# THE MAKE-BELIEVE MAN

## I

I HAD made up my mind that when my vacation came I would spend it seeking adventures. I have always wished for adventures, but, though I am old enough—I was twenty-five last October—and have always gone half-way to meet them, adventures avoid me. Kinney says it is my fault. He holds that if you want adventures you must go after them.

Kinney sits next to me at Joyce & Carboy's, the woollen manufacturers, where I am a stenographer, and Kinney is a clerk, and we both have rooms at Mrs. Shaw's boarding-house. Kinney is only a year older than myself, but he is always meeting with adventures. At night, when I have sat up late reading law, so that I may fit myself for court reporting, and in the hope that some day I may become a member of the bar, he will knock at my door and tell me some surprising thing that has just happened to him. Sometimes he has followed a fire-engine and helped people from a fire-escape, or he has pulled the shield off a policeman, or at the bar of the

Hotel Knickerbocker has made friends with a stranger, who turns out to be no less than a nobleman or an actor. And women, especially beautiful women, are always pursuing Kinney in taxicabs and calling upon him for assistance. Just to look at Kinney, without knowing how clever he is at getting people out of their difficulties, he does not appear to be a man to whom you would turn in time of trouble. You would think women in distress would appeal to some one bigger and stronger; would sooner ask a policeman. But, on the contrary, it is to Kinney that women always run, especially, as I have said, beautiful women. Nothing of the sort ever happens to me. I suppose, as Kinney says, it is because he was born and brought up in New York City and looks and acts like a New York man, while I, until a year ago, have always lived at Fairport. Fairport is a very pretty harbor, but it does not train one for adventures. We arranged to take our vacation at the same time, and together. At least Kinney so arranged it. I see a good deal of him, and in looking forward to my vacation, not the least pleasant feature of it was that everything connected with Joyce & Carboy and Mrs. Shaw's boarding-house would be left behind me. But when Kinney proposed we should go together, I could not see how, without being rude, I could refuse his company, and when he pointed out that for an expedition in search of adventure I could not select a better guide, I felt that he was right.

"Sometimes," he said, "I can see you don't believe that half the things I tell you have happened to me, really have happened. Now, isn't that so?"

To find the answer that would not hurt his feelings I hesitated, but he did not wait for my answer. He seldom does.

"Well, on this trip," he went on, "you will see Kinney on the job. You won't have to take my word for it. You will see adventures walk up and eat out of my hand."

Our vacation came on the first of September, but we began to plan for it in April, and up to the night before we left New York we never ceased planning. Our difficulty was that having been brought up at Fairport, which is on the Sound, north of New London, I was homesick for a smell of salt marshes and for the sight of water and ships. Though they were only schooners carrying cement, I wanted to sit in the sun on the string-piece of a wharf and watch them. I wanted to beat about the harbor in a catboat, and feel the tug and pull of the tiller. Kinney protested that that was no way to spend a vacation or to invite adventure. His face was set against Fairport. The conversation of clam-diggers, he said, did not appeal to him; and he complained that at Fairport our only chance of adventure would be my capsizing the catboat or robbing a lobster-pot. He insisted we should go to the mountains, where we would meet what he always calls "our best people." In September, he explained, everybody goes to the mountains to recuperate after the enervating atmosphere of the sea-shore. To this I objected that the little sea air we had inhaled at Mrs. Shaw's basement dining-room and in the sub-way need cause us no anxiety. And so, along these lines, throughout the sleepless, sultry nights of June, July, and August, we fought it out. There was not a summer resort within five hundred miles of New York City we did not consider. From the information bureaus and passenger agents of every railroad leaving New York, Kinney procured a library of time-tables, maps, folders, and pamphlets, illustrated with the most attractive pictures of summer hotels, golf links, tennis courts, and boat-houses. For two months he carried on a correspondence with the proprietors of these hotels; and in comparing the different prices they asked him for suites of rooms and sun parlors derived constant satisfaction.

"The Outlook House," he would announce,

"wants twenty-four dollars a day for bedroom, parlor, and private bath. While for the same accommodations the Carteret Arms asks only twenty. But the Carteret has no tennis court; and then again, the Outlook has no garage, nor are dogs allowed in the bedrooms."

As Kinney could not play lawn tennis, and as neither of us owned an automobile or a dog, or twenty-four dollars, these details to me seemed superfluous, but there was no health in pointing that out to Kinney. Because, as he himself says, he has so vivid an imagination that what he lacks he can "make believe" he has, and the pleasure of possession is his.

Kinney gives a great deal of thought to his clothes, and the question of what he should wear on his vacation was upon his mind. When I said I thought it was nothing to worry about, he snorted indignantly. "*You* wouldn't!" he said. "If *I'd* been brought up in a catboat, and had a tan like a red Indian, and hair like a Broadway blonde, I wouldn't worry either. Mrs. Shaw says you look exactly like a British peer in disguise." I had never seen a British peer, with or without his disguise, and I admit I was interested.

"Why are the girls in this house," demanded Kinney, "always running to your room to borrow matches? Because they admire your *clothes?*

If they're crazy about clothes, why don't they come to *me* for matches?"

"You are always out at night," I said.

"You know that's not the answer," he protested. "Why do the typewriter girls at the office always go to *you* to sharpen their pencils and tell them how to spell the hard words? Why do the girls in the lunch-rooms serve you first? Because they're hypnotized by your clothes? Is *that* it?"

"Do they?" I asked; "I hadn't noticed."

Kinney snorted and tossed up his arms. "He hadn't noticed!" he kept repeating. "He hadn't noticed!" For his vacation Kinney bought a second-hand suit-case. It was covered with labels of hotels in France and Switzerland.

"Joe," I said, "if you carry that bag you will be a walking falsehood."

Kinney's name is Joseph Forbes Kinney; he dropped the Joseph because he said it did not appear often enough in the *Social Register*, and could be found only in the Old Testament, and he has asked me to call him Forbes. Having first known him as "Joe," I occasionally forget.

"My name is *not* Joe," he said sternly, "and I have as much right to carry a second-hand bag as a new one. The bag says *it* has been to Europe. It does not say that *I* have been there."

"But, you probably will," I pointed out, "and then some one who has really visited those places——"

"Listen!" commanded Kinney. "If you want adventures you must be somebody of importance. No one will go shares in an adventure with Joe Kinney, a twenty-dollar-a-week clerk, the human adding machine, the hall-room boy. But Forbes Kinney, Esq., with a bag from Europe, and a Harvard ribbon round his hat——"

"Is that a Harvard ribbon round your hat?" I asked.

"It is!" declared Kinney; "and I have a Yale ribbon, and a Turf Club ribbon, too. They come on hooks, and you hook 'em on to match your clothes, or the company you keep. And, what's more," he continued, with some heat, "I've borrowed a tennis racket and a golf bag full of sticks, and you take care you don't give me away."

"I see," I returned, "that you are going to get us into a lot of trouble."

"I was thinking," said Kinney, looking at me rather doubtfully, "it might help a lot if for the first week you acted as my secretary, and during the second week I was your secretary."

Sometimes, when Mr. Joyce goes on a business trip, he takes me with him as his private stenographer, and the change from office work is very pleasant; but I could not see why I should spend one week of my holiday writing letters for Kinney.

"You wouldn't write any letters," he explained. "But if I could tell people you were my private secretary, it would naturally give me a certain importance.

"If it will make you any happier," I said, "you can tell people I am a British peer in disguise."

"There is no use in being nasty about it," protested Kinney. "I am only trying to show you a way that would lead to adventure."

"It surely would!" I assented. "It would lead us to jail."

The last week in August came, and, as to where we were to go we still were undecided, I suggested we leave it to chance.

"The first thing," I pointed out, "is to get away from this awful city. The second thing is to get away cheaply. Let us write down the names of the summer resorts to which we can travel by rail or by boat for two dollars and put them in a hat. The name of the place we draw will be the one for which we start Saturday afternoon. The idea," I urged, "is in itself full of adventure."

Kinney agreed, but reluctantly. What chiefly disturbed him was the thought that the places near New York to which one could travel for so little money were not likely to be fashionable.

"I have a terrible fear," he declared, "that, with this limit of yours, we will wake up in Asbury Park."

Friday night came and found us prepared for departure, and at midnight we held our lottery. In a pillow-case we placed twenty slips of paper, on each of which was written the name of a summer resort. Ten of these places were selected by Kinney, and ten by myself. Kinney dramatically rolled up his sleeve, and, plunging his bared arm into our grab-bag, drew out a slip of paper and read aloud: "New Bedford, via New Bedford Steamboat Line." The choice was one of mine.

"New Bedford!" shouted Kinney. His tone expressed the keenest disappointment. "It's a mill town!" he exclaimed. "It's full of cotton mills."

"That may be," I protested. "But it's also a most picturesque old seaport, one of the oldest in America. You can see whaling vessels at the wharfs there, and wooden figure-heads, and harpoons——"

"Is this an expedition to dig up buried cities," interrupted Kinney, "or a pleasure trip? I don't *want* to see harpoons! I wouldn't know a harpoon if you stuck one into me. I prefer to see hatpins."

# THE MAKE-BELIEVE MAN

The *Patience* did not sail until six o'clock, but we were so anxious to put New York behind us that at five we were on board. Our cabin was an outside one with two berths. After placing our suit-cases in it, we collected camp-chairs and settled ourselves in a cool place on the boat deck. Kinney had bought all the afternoon papers, and, as later I had reason to remember, was greatly interested over the fact that the young Earl of Ivy had at last arrived in this country. For some weeks the papers had been giving more space than seemed necessary to that young Irishman and to the young lady he was coming over to marry. There had been pictures of his different country houses, pictures of himself; in uniform, in the robes he wore at the coronation, on a polo pony, as Master of Fox-hounds. And there had been pictures of Miss Aldrich, and of *her* country places at Newport and on the Hudson. From the afternoon papers Kinney learned that, having sailed under his family name of Meehan, the young man and Lady Moya, his sister, had that morning landed in New York, but before the reporters had discovered them, had escaped from the wharf and disappeared.

"'Inquiries at the different hotels,'" read Kinney impressively, "'failed to establish the whereabouts of his lordship and Lady Moya, and it is believed they at once left by train for Newport.'"

With awe Kinney pointed at the red funnels of the *Mauretania*.

"There is the boat that brought them to America," he said. "I see," he added, "that in this picture of him playing golf he wears one of those knit jackets the Eiselbaum has just marked down to three dollars and seventy-five cents. I wish—" he added regretfully.

"You can get one at New Bedford," I suggested.

"I wish," he continued, "we had gone to Newport. All of our *best* people will be there for the wedding. It is the most important social event of the season. You might almost call it an alliance."

I went forward to watch them take on the freight, and Kinney stationed himself at the rail above the passengers' gangway where he could see the other passengers arrive. He had dressed himself with much care, and was wearing his Yale hat-band, but when a very smart-looking youth came up the gangplank wearing a Harvard ribbon, Kinney hastily retired to our cabin and returned with one like it. A few minutes later I found him and the young man seated in camp-chairs side by side engaged in a conversation in which Kinney seemed to bear the greater part.

Indeed, to what Kinney was saying the young man paid not the slightest attention. Instead, his eyes were fastened on the gangplank below, and when a young man of his own age, accompanied by a girl in a dress of rough tweed, appeared upon it, he leaped from his seat. Then with a conscious look at Kinney, sank back.

The girl in the tweed suit was sufficiently beautiful to cause any man to rise and to remain standing. She was the most beautiful girl I had ever seen. She had gray eyes and hair like golden-rod, worn in a fashion with which I was not familiar, and her face was so lovely that in my surprise at the sight of it, I felt a sudden catch at my throat, and my heart stopped with awe, and wonder, and gratitude.

After a brief moment the young man in the real Harvard hat-band rose restlessly and, with a nod to Kinney, went below. I also rose and followed him. I had an uncontrollable desire to again look at the girl with the golden-rod hair. I did not mean that she should see me. Never before had I done such a thing. But never before had I seen any one who had moved me so strangely. Seeking her, I walked the length of the main saloon and back again, but could not find her. The delay gave me time to see that my conduct was impertinent. The very fact that she was so lovely to look upon should have been her protection. It afforded me no excuse to follow and spy upon her. With this thought, I hastily returned to the upper deck to bury myself in my book. If it did not serve to keep my mind from the young lady, at least I would prevent my eyes from causing her annoyance.

I was about to take the chair that the young man had left vacant when Kinney objected.

"He was very much interested in our conversation," Kinney said, "and he may return."

I had not noticed any eagerness on the part of the young man to talk to Kinney or to listen to him, but I did not sit down.

"I should not be surprised a bit," said Kinney, "if that young man is no end of a swell. He is a Harvard man, and his manner was most polite. That," explained Kinney, "is one way you can always tell a real swell. They're not high and mighty with you. Their social position is so secure that they can do as they like. For instance, did you notice that he smoked a pipe?"

I said I had not noticed it.

For his holiday Kinney had purchased a box of cigars of a quality more expensive than those he can usually afford. He was smoking one of them at the moment, and, as it grew less, had been carefully moving the gold band with which it was encircled from the lighted end. But as he spoke he regarded it apparently with distaste, and then dropped it overboard.

"Keep my chair," he said, rising. "I am going to my cabin to get my pipe." I sat down and fastened my eyes upon my book; but neither did I understand what I was reading nor see the printed page. Instead, before my eyes, confusing and blinding me, was the lovely, radiant face of the beautiful lady. In perplexity I looked up, and found her standing not two feet from me. Something pulled me out of my chair. Something made me move it toward her. I lifted my hat and backed away. But the eyes of the lovely lady halted me.

To my perplexity, her face expressed both surprise and pleasure. It was as though either she thought she knew me, or that I reminded her of some man she did know. Were the latter the case, he must have been a friend, for the way in which she looked at me was kind. And there was, besides, the expression of surprise and as though something she saw pleased her. Maybe it was the quickness with which I had offered my chair. Still looking at me, she pointed to one of the sky-scrapers.

"Could you tell me," she asked, "the name of that building?" Had her question not proved it, her voice would have told me not only that she was a stranger, but that she was Irish. It was particularly soft, low, and vibrant. It made the commonplace question she asked sound as though she had sung it. I told her the name of the building, and that farther uptown, as she would see when we moved into midstream, there was another still taller. She listened, regarding me brightly, as though interested; but before her I was embarrassed, and, fearing I intruded, I again made a movement to go away. With another question she stopped me. I could see no reason for her doing so, but it was almost as though she had asked the question only to detain me.

"What is that odd boat," she said, "pumping water into the river?"

I explained that it was a fire-boat testing her hose-lines, and then as we moved into the channel I gained courage, and found myself pointing out the Statue of Liberty, Governor's Island, and the Brooklyn Bridge. The fact that it was a stranger who was talking did not seem to disturb her. I cannot tell how she conveyed the idea, but I soon felt that she felt, no matter what unconventional thing she chose to do, people would not be rude, or misunderstand.

I considered telling her my name. At first it seemed that that would be more polite. Then I saw to do so would be forcing myself upon her, that she was interested in me only as a guide to New York Harbor.

When we passed the Brooklyn Navy Yard I talked so much and so eagerly of the battle-ships at anchor there that the lady must have thought I had followed the sea, for she asked: "Are you a sailorman?"

It was the first question that was in any way personal.

"I used to sail a catboat," I said.

My answer seemed to puzzle her, and she frowned. Then she laughed delightedly, like one having made a discovery.

"You don't say 'sailorman,'" she said. "What do you ask, over here, when you want to know if a man is in the navy?"

She spoke as though we were talking a different language.

"We ask if he is in the navy," I answered.

She laughed again at that, quite as though I had said something clever.

"And you are not?"

"No," I said, "I am in Joyce & Carboy's office. I am a stenographer."

Again my answer seemed both to puzzle and to surprise her. She regarded me doubtfully. I could see that she thought, for some reason, I was misleading her.

"In an office?" she repeated. Then, as though she had caught me, she said: "How do you keep so fit?" She asked the question directly, as a man would have asked it, and as she spoke I was conscious that her eyes were measuring me and my shoulders, as though she were wondering to what weight I could strip.

"It's only lately I've worked in an office," I said. "Before that I always worked out-of-doors; oystering and clamming and, in the fall, scalloping. And in the summer I played ball on a hotel nine."

I saw that to the beautiful lady my explanation carried no meaning whatsoever, but before I could explain, the young man with whom she had come on board walked toward us.

Neither did he appear to find in her talking to a stranger anything embarrassing. He halted and smiled. His smile was pleasant, but entirely vague. In the few minutes I was with him, I learned that it was no sign that he was secretly pleased. It was merely his expression. It was as though a photographer had said: "Smile, please," and he had smiled.

When he joined us, out of deference to the young lady I raised my hat, but the youth did not seem to think that outward show of respect was necessary, and kept his hands in his pockets.

Neither did he cease smoking. His first remark to the lovely lady somewhat startled me.

"Have you got a brass bed in your room?" he asked. The beautiful lady said she had.

"So've I," said the young man. "They do you rather well, don't they? And it's only three dollars. How much is that?"

"Four times three would be twelve," said the lady. "Twelve shillings."

The young man was smoking a cigarette in a long amber cigarette-holder. I never had seen one so long. He examined the end of his cigarette-holder, and, apparently surprised and relieved at finding a cigarette there, again smiled contentedly.

The lovely lady pointed at the marble shaft rising above Madison Square.

"That is the tallest sky-scraper," she said, "in New York." I had just informed her of that fact. The young man smiled as though he were being introduced to the building, but exhibited no interest.

"*Is* it?" he remarked. His tone seemed to show that had she said, "That is a rabbit," he would have been equally gratified.

"Some day," he stated, with the same startling abruptness with which he had made his first remark, "our war-ships will lift the roofs off those sky-scrapers."

The remark struck me in the wrong place. It was unnecessary. Already I resented the manner of the young man toward the lovely lady. It seemed to me lacking in courtesy. He knew her, and yet treated her with no deference, while I, a stranger, felt so grateful to her for being what I knew one with such a face must be, that I could have knelt at her feet. So I rather resented the remark.

"If the war-ships you send over here," I said doubtfully, "aren't more successful in lifting things than your yachts, you'd better keep them at home and save coal!"

Seldom have I made so long a speech or so rude a speech, and as soon as I had spoken, on account of the lovely lady, I was sorry.

But after a pause of half a second she laughed delightedly.

"I see," she cried, as though it were a sort of a game. "He means Lipton! We can't lift the cup, we can't lift the roofs. Don't you see, Stumps?" she urged. In spite of my rude remark, the young man she called Stumps had continued to smile happily. Now his expression changed to one of discomfort and utter gloom, and then broke out into a radiant smile.

"I say!" he cried. "That's awfully good: 'If your war-ships aren't any better at lifting things—' Oh, I say, really," he protested, "that's awfully good." He seemed to be afraid I would not appreciate the rare excellence of my speech. "You know, really," he pleaded, "it is *awfully* good!"

We were interrupted by the sudden appearance, in opposite directions, of Kinney and the young man with the real hat-band. Both were excited and disturbed. At the sight of the young man, Stumps turned appealingly to the golden-rod girl. He groaned aloud, and his expression was that of a boy who had been caught playing truant.

"Oh, Lord!" he exclaimed, "what's he huffy about now? He *told* me I could come on deck as soon as we started."

The girl turned upon me a sweet and lovely smile and nodded. Then, with Stumps at her side, she moved to meet the young man. When he saw them coming he halted, and, when they joined him, began talking earnestly, almost angrily. As he did so, much to my bewilderment, he glared at me. At the same moment Kinney grabbed me by the arm.

"Come below!" he commanded. His tone was hoarse and thrilling with excitement.

"Our adventures," he whispered, "have begun!"

## II

I FELT, for me, adventures had already begun, for my meeting with the beautiful lady was the event of my life, and though Kinney and I had agreed to share our adventures, of this one I knew I could not even speak to him. I wanted to be alone, where I could delight in it, where I could go over what she had said; what I had said. I would share it with no one. It was too wonderful, too sacred. But Kinney would not be denied. He led me to our cabin and locked the door.

"I am sorry," he began, "but this adventure is one I cannot share with you." The remark was so in keeping with my own thoughts that with sudden unhappy doubt I wondered if Kinney, too, had felt the charm of the beautiful lady. But he quickly undeceived me.

"I have been doing a little detective work," he said. His voice was low and sepulchral. "And I have come upon a real adventure. There are reasons why I cannot share it with you, but as it develops you can follow it. About half an hour ago," he explained, "I came here to get my pipe. The window was open. The lattice was only partly closed. Outside was that young man from Harvard who tried to make my acquaintance, and the young Englishman who came on board with that blonde." Kinney suddenly interrupted himself. "You were talking to her just now," he said. I hated to hear him speak of the Irish lady as "that blonde." I hated to hear him speak of her at all. So, to shut him off, I answered briefly: "She asked me about the Singer Building."

"I see," said Kinney. "Well, these two men were just outside my window, and, while I was searching for my pipe, I heard the American speaking. He was very excited and angry. 'I tell you,' he said, 'every boat and railroad station is watched. You won't be safe till we get away from New York. You must go to your cabin and *stay* there.' And the other one answered: 'I am sick of hiding and dodging.'"

Kinney paused dramatically and frowned.

"Well," I asked, "what of it?"

"What of it?" he cried. He exclaimed aloud with pity and impatience.

"No wonder," he cried, "you never have adventures. Why, it's plain as print. They are criminals escaping. The Englishman certainly is escaping."

I was concerned only for the lovely lady, but

247

I asked: "You mean the Irishman called Stumps?"

"Stumps!" exclaimed Kinney. "What a strange name. Too strange to be true. It's an alias!" I was incensed that Kinney should charge the friends of the lovely lady with being criminals. Had it been any one else I would have at once resented it, but to be angry with Kinney is difficult. I could not help but remember that he is the slave of his own imagination. It plays tricks and runs away with him. And if it leads him to believe innocent people are criminals, it also leads him to believe that every woman in the subway to whom he gives his seat is a great lady, a leader of society on her way to work in the slums.

"Joe!" I protested. "Those men aren't criminals. I talked to that Irishman, and he hasn't sense enough to be a criminal."

"The railroads are watched," repeated Kinney. "Do *honest* men care a darn whether the railroad is watched or not? Do you care? Do I care? And did you notice how angry the American got when he found Stumps talking with you?"

I had noticed it; and I also recalled the fact that Stumps had said to the lovely lady: "He told me I could come on deck as soon as we started."

The words seemed to bear out what Kinney claimed he had overheard. But not wishing to encourage him, of what I had heard I said nothing.

"He may be dodging a summons," I suggested. "He is wanted, probably, only as a witness. It might be a civil suit, or his chauffeur may have hit somebody."

Kinney shook his head sadly.

"Excuse me," he said, "but I fear you lack imagination. Those men are rascals, dangerous rascals, and the woman is their accomplice. What they have done I don't know, but I have already learned enough to arrest them as suspicious characters. Listen! Each of them has a separate state-room forward. The window of the American's room was open, and his suit-case was on the bed. On it were the initials H. P. A. The state-room is number twenty-four, but when I examined the purser's list, pretending I wished to find out if a friend of mine was on board, I found that the man in twenty-four had given his name as James Preston. Now," he demanded, "why should one of them hide under an alias and the other be afraid to show himself until we leave the wharf?" He did not wait for my answer. "I have been talking to Mr. H. P. A., *alias* Preston," he continued. "I pretended I was a person of some importance. I hinted I was rich. My object," Kinney added hastily, "was to encourage him to try some of his tricks on *me;* to try to rob *me;* so that I could obtain evidence. I also," he went on, with some embarrassment, "told him that you, too, were wealthy and of some importance."

I thought of the lovely lady, and I felt myself blushing indignantly.

"You did very wrong," I cried; "you had no right! You may involve us both most unpleasantly."

"You are not involved in any way," protested Kinney. "As soon as we reach New Bedford you can slip on shore and wait for me at the hotel. When I've finished with these gentlemen, I'll join you."

"Finished with them!" I exclaimed. "What do you mean to do to them?"

"Arrest them!" cried Kinney sternly, "as soon as they step upon the wharf!"

"You can't do it!" I gasped.

"I *have* done it!" answered Kinney. "It's good as done. I have notified the chief of police at New Bedford," he declared proudly, "to meet me at the wharf. I used the wireless. Here is my message."

From his pocket he produced a paper and, with great importance, read aloud: "Meet me at wharf on arrival steamer *Patience*. Two well-known criminals on board escaping New York police. Will personally lay charges against them.—Forbes Kinney."

As soon as I could recover from my surprise, I made violent protest. I pointed out to Kinney that his conduct was outrageous, that in making such serious charges, on such evidence, he would lay himself open to punishment.

He was not in the least dismayed.

"I take it then," he said importantly, "that you do not wish to appear against them?"

"I don't wish to appear in it at all!" I cried. "You've no right to annoy that young lady. You must wire the police you are mistaken."

"I have no desire to arrest the woman," said Kinney stiffly. "In my message I did not mention *her*. If you want an adventure of your own, you might help her to escape while I arrest her accomplices."

"I object," I cried, "to your applying the word 'accomplice' to that young lady. And suppose they *are* criminals," I demanded, "how will arresting them help you?"

Kinney's eyes flashed with excitement.

"Think of the newspapers," he cried; "they'll be full of it!" Already in imagination he saw the headlines. " 'A Clever Haul!'" he quoted. " 'Noted band of crooks elude New York police, but are captured by Forbes Kinney.'" He sighed contentedly. "And they'll probably print my picture, too," he added.

I knew I should be angry with him, but instead I could only feel sorry. I have known Kinney for a year, and I have learned that his "make-believe" is always innocent. I suppose that he is what is called a snob, but with him snobbishness is not an unpleasant weakness. In his case it takes the form of thinking that people who have certain things he does not possess are better than himself; and that, therefore, they must be worth knowing, and he tries to make their acquaintance. But he does not think that he himself is better than any one. His life is very bare and narrow. In consequence, on many things he places false values. As, for example, his desire to see his name in the newspapers even as an amateur detective. So, while I was indignant I also was sorry.

"Joe," I said, "you're going to get yourself into an awful lot of trouble, and though I am not in this adventure, you know if I can help you I will."

He thanked me and we went to the dining-saloon. There, at a table near ours, we saw the lovely lady and Stumps and the American. She again smiled at me, but this time, so it seemed, a little doubtfully.

# THE MAKE-BELIEVE MAN

In the mind of the American, on the contrary, there was no doubt. He glared both at Kinney and myself, as though he would like to boil us in oil.

After dinner, in spite of my protests, Kinney set forth to interview him and, as he described it, to "lead him on" to commit himself. I feared Kinney was much more likely to commit himself than the other, and when I saw them seated together I watched from a distance with much anxiety.

An hour later, while I was alone, a steward told me the purser would like to see me. I went to his office, and found gathered there Stumps, his American friend, the night watchman of the boat, and the purser. As though inviting him to speak, the purser nodded to the American. That gentleman addressed me in an excited and belligerent manner.

"My name is Aldrich," he said; "I want to know what *your* name is?"

I did not quite like his tone, nor did I like being summoned to the purser's office to be questioned by a stranger.

"Why?" I asked.

"Because," said Aldrich, "it seems you have *several* names. As one of them belongs to *this* gentleman"—he pointed at Stumps—"he wants to know why you are using it."

I looked at Stumps and he greeted me with the vague and genial smile that was habitual to him, but on being caught in the act by Aldrich he hurriedly frowned.

"I have never used any name but my own," I said; "and," I added pleasantly, "if I were choosing a name I wouldn't choose 'Stumps,'"

Aldrich fairly gasped.

"His name is not Stumps!" he cried indignantly. "He is the Earl of Ivy!"

He evidently expected me to be surprised at this, and I *was* surprised. I stared at the much-advertised young Irishman with interest.

Aldrich misunderstood my silence, and in a triumphant tone, which was far from pleasant, continued: "So you see," he sneered, "when you chose to pass yourself off as Ivy you should have picked out another boat."

The thing was too absurd for me to be angry, and I demanded with patience: "But why should I pass myself off as Lord Ivy?"

"That's what we intend to find out," snapped Aldrich. "Anyway, we've stopped your game for to-night, and to-morrow you can explain to the police! Your pal," he taunted, "has told every one on this boat that you are Lord Ivy, and he's told me lies enough about *himself* to prove *he's* an impostor, too!"

I saw what had happened, and that if I were

to protect poor Kinney I must not, as I felt inclined, use my fists, but my head. I laughed with apparent unconcern, and turned to the purser.

"Oh, that's it, is it?" I cried. "I might have known it was Kinney; he's always playing practical jokes on me." I turned to Aldrich. "My friend has been playing a joke on you, too," I said. "He didn't know who you were, but he saw you were an Anglomaniac, and he's been having fun with you!"

"Has he?" roared Aldrich. He reached down into his pocket and pulled out a piece of paper. "This," he cried, shaking it at me, "is a copy of a wireless that I've just sent to the chief of police at New Bedford."

With great satisfaction he read it in a loud and threatening voice: "Two impostors on this boat representing themselves to be Lord Ivy, my future brother-in-law, and his secretary. Lord Ivy himself on board. Send police to meet boat. We will make charges.—Henry Philip Aldrich."

It occurred to me that after receiving two such sensational telegrams, and getting out of bed to meet the boat at six in the morning, the chief of police would be in a state of mind to arrest almost anybody, and that his choice would certainly fall on Kinney and myself. It was ridiculous, but it also was likely to prove extremely humiliating. So I said, speaking to Lord Ivy: "There's been a mistake all around; send for Mr. Kinney and I will explain it to you." Lord Ivy, who was looking extremely bored, smiled and nodded, but young Aldrich laughed ironically.

"Mr. Kinney is in his state-room," he said, "with a steward guarding the door and window. You can explain to-morrow to the police."

I rounded indignantly upon the purser.

"Are you keeping Mr. Kinney a prisoner in his state-room?" I demanded. "If you are——"

"He doesn't have to stay there," protested the purser sulkily. "When he found the stewards were following him he went to his cabin."

"I will see him at once," I said. "And if I catch any of your stewards following *me*, I'll drop them overboard."

No one tried to stop me—indeed, knowing I could not escape, they seemed pleased at my departure, and I went to my cabin.

Kinney, seated on the edge of the berth, greeted me with a hollow groan. His expression was one of utter misery. As though begging me not to be angry, he threw out his arms appealingly.

"How the devil!" he began, "was I to know that a little red-headed shrimp like that was the Earl of Ivy? And that that tall blond girl," he added indignantly, "that I thought was an accomplice, is Lady Moya, his sister?"

"What happened?" I asked.

Kinney was wearing his hat. He took it off and hurled it to the floor.

"It was that damned hat!" he cried. "It's a Harvard ribbon, all right, but only men on the crew can wear it! How was I to know *that?* I saw Aldrich looking at it in a puzzled way, and when he said, 'I see you are on the crew,' I guessed what it meant, and said I was on last year's crew. Unfortunately *he* was on last year's crew! That's what made him suspect me, and after dinner he put me through a third degree. I must have given the wrong answers, for suddenly he jumped up and called me a swindler and an impostor. I got back by telling him he was a crook and that I was a detective, and that I had sent a wireless to have him arrested at New Bedford. He challenged me to prove I was a detective, and, of course, I couldn't, and he called up two stewards and told them to watch me while he went after the purser. I didn't fancy being watched, so I came here."

"When did you tell him I was the Earl of Ivy?"

Kinney ran his fingers through his hair and groaned dismally.

"That was before the boat started," he said; "it was only a joke. He didn't seem to be interested in my conversation, so I thought I'd liven it up a bit by saying I was a friend of Lord Ivy's. And you happened to pass, and I happened to remember Mrs. Shaw saying you looked like a British peer, so I said: 'That is my friend Lord Ivy.' I said I was your secretary, and he seemed greatly interested, and—" Kinney added dismally, "I talked too much. I am *so* sorry," he begged. "It's going to be awful for you!" His eyes suddenly lit with hope. "Unless," he whispered, "we can escape!"

The same thought was in my mind, but the idea was absurd, and impracticable. I knew there was no escape. I knew we were sentenced at sunrise to a most humiliating and disgraceful experience. The newspapers would regard anything that concerned Lord Ivy as news. In my turn I also saw the hideous head-lines. What would my father and mother at Fairport think; what would my old friends there think; and, what was of even greater importance, how would Joyce & Carboy act? What chance was there left me, after I had been arrested as an impostor, to become a stenographer in the law courts —in time, a member of the bar? But I found that what, for the moment, distressed me most was that the lovely lady would consider me a knave or a fool. The thought made me exclaim with exasperation. Had it been possible to abandon Kinney, I would have dropped overboard and made for shore. The night was warm and foggy, and the short journey to land, to one who had been brought up like a duck, meant nothing more than a wetting. But I did not see how I could desert Kinney.

"Can you swim?" I asked.

"Of course not!" he answered gloomily; "and, besides," he added, "our names are on our suit-cases. We couldn't take them with us, and they'd find out who we are. If we could only steal a boat!" he exclaimed eagerly— "one of those on the davits," he urged—"we could put our suit-cases in it and then, after every one is asleep, we could lower it into the water."

The smallest boat on board was certified to hold twenty-five persons, and without waking the entire ship's company we could as easily have moved the chart-room. This I pointed out.

"Don't make objections!" Kinney cried petulantly. He was rapidly recovering his spirits. The imminence of danger seemed to inspire him.

"Think!" he commanded. "Think of some

way by which we can get off this boat before she reaches New Bedford. We *must!* We must not be arrested! It would be too awful!" He interrupted himself with an excited exclamation.

"I have it!" he whispered hoarsely: "I will ring in the fire-alarm! The crew will run to quarters. The boats will be lowered. We will cut one of them adrift. In the confusion——"

What was to happen in the confusion that his imagination had conjured up, I was not to know. For what actually happened was so confused that of nothing am I quite certain. First, from the water of the Sound, that was lapping pleasantly against the side, I heard the voice of a man raised in terror. Then came a rush of feet, oaths, and yells; then a shock that threw us to our knees, and a crunching, ripping, and tearing roar like that made by the roof of a burning building when it plunges to the cellar.

And the next instant a large bowsprit entered our cabin window. There was left me just space enough to wrench the door open, and grabbing Kinney, who was still on his knees, I dragged him into the alleyway. He scrambled upright and clasped his hands to his head.

"Where's my hat?" he cried.

I could hear the water pouring into the lower deck and sweeping the freight and trunks before it. A horse in a box stall was squealing like a human being, and many human beings were screaming and shrieking like animals. My first intelligent thought was of the lovely lady. I shook Kinney by the arm. The uproar was so great that to make him hear I was forced to shout. "Where is Lord Ivy's cabin?" I cried. "You said it's next to his sister's. Take me there!"

Kinney nodded, and ran down the corridor and into an alleyway on which opened three cabins. The doors were ajar, and as I looked into each I saw that the beds had not been touched, and that the cabins were empty. I knew then that she was still on deck. I felt that I must find her. We ran toward the companionway.

"Women and children first!" Kinney was yelling. "Women and children first!" As we raced down the slanting floor of the saloon he kept repeating this mechanically. At that moment the electric lights went out, and, except for the oil lamps, the ship was in darkness. Many of the passengers had already gone to bed. These now burst from the state-rooms in strange garments, carrying life-preservers, hand-bags, their arms full of clothing. One man in one hand clutched a sponge, in the other an umbrella. With this he beat at those who blocked his flight. He hit a woman over the head, and I hit him and he went down. Finding himself on his knees, he began to pray volubly.

When we reached the upper deck we pushed out of the crush at the gangway and, to keep our footing, for there was a strong list to port, clung to the big flag-staff at the stern. At each rail the crew were swinging the boats over the side, and around each boat was a crazy, fighting mob. Above our starboard rail towered the foremast of a schooner. She had rammed us fair amidships, and in her bows was a hole through which you could have rowed a boat. Into this the water was rushing and sucking her down. She was already settling at the stern. By the light of a swinging lantern I saw three of her crew lift a yawl from her deck and lower it into the water. Into it they hurled oars and a sail, and one of them had already started to slide down the painter when the schooner lurched drunkenly; and in a panic all three of the men ran forward and leaped to our lower deck. The yawl, abandoned, swung idly between the *Patience* and the schooner. Kinney, seeing what I saw, grabbed me by the arm.

"There!" he whispered, pointing; "there's our chance!" I saw that, with safety, the yawl could hold a third person, and as to who the third passenger would be I had already made up my mind.

"Wait here!" I said.

On the *Patience* there were many immigrants, only that afternoon released from Ellis Island. They had swarmed into the life-boats even before they were swung clear, and when the ship's officers drove them off, the poor souls, not being able to understand, believed they were being sacrificed for the safety of the other passengers. So each was fighting, as he thought, for his life and for the lives of his wife and children. At the edge of the scrimmage I dragged out two women who had been knocked off their feet and who were in danger of being trampled. But neither was the woman I sought. In the half-darkness I saw one of the immigrants, a girl with a 'kerchief on her head, struggling with her life-belt. A stoker, as he raced past, seized it and made for the rail. In my turn I took it from him, and he fought for it, shouting: "It's every man for himself now!"

"All right," I said, for I was excited and angry, "look out for *yourself* then!" I hit him on the chin, and he let go of the life-belt and dropped.

I heard at my elbow a low, excited laugh, and a voice said: "Well bowled! You never learned that in an office." I turned and saw the lovely lady. I tossed the immigrant girl her life-belt, and as though I had known Lady Moya all my life I took her by the hand and dragged her after me down the deck.

"You come with me!" I commanded. I found that I was trembling and that a weight of anxiety of which I had not been conscious had been lifted. I found I was still holding her hand and pressing it in my own. "Thank God!" I said. "I thought I had lost you!"

"Lost me!" repeated Lady Moya. But she made no comment. "I must find my brother," she said.

"You must come with me!" I ordered. "Go with Mr. Kinney to the lower deck. I will bring that rowboat under the stern. You will jump into it."

"I cannot leave my brother!" said Lady Moya.

Upon the word, as though shot from a cannon, the human whirlpool that was sweeping the deck amidships cast out Stumps and hurled him toward us. His sister gave a little cry of relief. Stumps recovered his balance and shook himself like a dog that has been in the water.

"Thought I'd never get out of it alive!" he remarked complacently. In the darkness I could not see his face, but I was sure he was still vaguely smiling. "Worse than a foot-ball night!" he exclaimed; "worse than Mafeking night!"

His sister pointed to the yawl.

"This gentleman is going to bring that boat here and take us away in it," she told him. "We had better go when we can!"

"Right ho!" assented Stumps cheerfully. "How about Phil? He's just behind me."

As he spoke, only a few yards from us a peevish voice pierced the tumult.

"I tell you," it cried, "you must find Lord Ivy! If Lord Ivy——"

A voice with a strong and brutal American accent yelled in answer: "To hell with Lord Ivy!"

Lady Moya chuckled.

"Get to the lower deck!" I commanded. "I am going for the yawl."

As I slipped my leg over the rail I heard Lord Ivy say: "I'll find Phil and meet you."

I dropped and caught the rail of the deck below, and, hanging from it, shoved with my knees and fell into the water. Two strokes brought me to the yawl, and, scrambling into her and casting her off, I paddled back to the steamer. As I lay under the stern I heard from the lower deck the voice of Kinney raised importantly.

"Ladies first!" he cried. "Her ladyship first, I mean," he corrected. Even on leaving what he believed to be a sinking ship, Kinney could not forget his manners. But Mr. Aldrich had evidently forgotten his. I heard him shout indignantly: "I'll be damned if I do!"

The voice of Lady Moya laughed.

"You'll be drowned if you don't!" she answered. I saw a black shadow poised upon the rail. "Steady below there!" her voice called, and the next moment, as lightly as a squirrel, she dropped to the thwart and stumbled into my arms.

The voice of Aldrich was again raised in anger. "I'd rather drown!" he cried.

Lord Ivy responded with unexpected spirit.

"Well, then, drown! The water is warm and it's a pleasing death."

At that, with a bump, he fell in a heap at my feet.

"Easy, Kinney!" I shouted. "Don't swamp us!"

"I'll be careful!" he called, and the next instant hit my shoulders and I shook him off on top of Lord Ivy.

"Get off my head!" shouted his lordship.

Kinney apologized to every one profusely. Lady Moya raised her voice.

"For the last time, Phil," she called, "are you coming or are you not?"

"Not with those swindlers, I'm not!" he shouted. "I think you two are mad! I prefer to drown!"

There was an uncomfortable silence. My position was a difficult one, and, not knowing what to say, I said nothing.

"If one must drown!" exclaimed Lady Moya briskly, "I can't see it matters who one drowns with."

In his strangely explosive manner Lord Ivy shouted suddenly: "Phil, you're a silly ass."

"Push off!" commanded Lady Moya.

I think, from her tone, the order was given more for the benefit of Aldrich than for myself. Certainly it was effective, for on the instant there was a heavy splash. Lord Ivy sniffed scornfully and manifested no interest.

"Ah!" he exclaimed, "he prefers to drown!"

Sputtering and gasping, Aldrich rose out of the water and, while we balanced the boat, climbed over the side.

"Understand!" he cried even while he was still gasping, "I am here under protest. I am here to protect you and Stumps. I am under obligation to no one. I'm——"

"Can you row?" I asked.

"Why don't you ask your pal?" he demanded savagely; "he rowed on last year's crew."

"Phil!" cried Lady Moya. Her voice suggested a temper I had not suspected. "You will row or you can get out and walk! Take the oars," she commanded, "and be civil!"

Lady Moya, with the tiller in her hand, sat in the stern; Stumps, with Kinney huddled at his knees, was stowed away forward. I took the stroke and Aldrich the bow oars.

"We will make for the Connecticut shore," I said, and pulled from under the stern of the *Patience.*

In a few minutes we had lost all sight and, except for her whistle, all sound of her; and we ourselves were lost in the fog. There was another eloquent and embarrassing silence. Unless, in the panic, they trampled upon each other, I had no real fear for the safety of those on board the steamer. Before we had abandoned her I had heard the wireless frantically sputtering the "stand-by" call, and I was certain that already the big boats of the Fall River, Providence, and Joy lines, and launches from every wireless station between Bridgeport and Newport, were making toward her. But the margin of safety, which to my thinking was broad enough for all the other passengers, for the lovely lady was in no way sufficient. That mob-swept deck was no place for her. I was happy that, on her account, I had not waited for a possible rescue. In the yawl she was safe. The water was smooth, and the Connecticut shore was, I judged, not more than three miles distant. In an hour, unless the fog confused us, I felt sure the lovely lady would again walk safely upon dry land. Selfishly, on Kinney's account and my own, I was delighted to find myself free of the steamer, and from any chance of her landing us where police waited with open arms. The avenging angel in the person of Aldrich was still near us, so near that I could hear the water dripping from his clothes, but his power to harm was gone. I was congratulating myself on this when suddenly he undeceived me. Apparently he had been considering his position toward Kinney and myself, and, having arrived at a conclusion, was anxious to announce it.

"I wish to repeat," he exclaimed suddenly, "that I'm under obligations to nobody. Just because my friends," he went on defiantly, "choose to trust themselves with persons who ought to be in jail, I can't desert them. It's all the more reason why I *shouldn't* desert them. That's why I'm here! And I want it understood as soon as I get on shore I'm going to a police station and have those persons arrested."

Rising out of the fog that had rendered each of us invisible to the other, his words sounded fantastic and unreal. In the dripping silence, broken only by hoarse warnings that came from no direction, and within the mind of each the conviction that we were lost, police stations did not immediately concern us. So no one spoke, and in the fog the words died away and were drowned. But I was glad he had spoken. At least I was forewarned. I now knew that I had not escaped, that Kinney and I were still in danger. I determined that so far as it lay with me, our yawl would be beached at that point of the coast of Connecticut farthest removed, not only from police stations, but from all human habitation.

As soon as we were out of hearing of the *Patience* and her whistle, we completely lost our bearings. It may be that Lady Moya was not a skilled coxswain, or it may be that Aldrich understands a racing scull better than a yawl, and pulled too heavily on his right, but whatever the cause we soon were hopelessly lost. In this predicament we were not alone. The night was filled with fog-horns, whistles, bells, and the throb of engines, but we never were near enough to hail the vessels from which the sounds came, and when we rowed toward them they invariably sank into silence. After two hours Stumps and Kinney insisted on taking a turn at the oars, and Lady Moya moved to the bow. We gave her our coats, and, making cushions of these, she announced that she was going to sleep. Whether she slept or not, I do not know, but she remained silent. For three more dreary hours we took turns at the oars or dozed at the bottom of the boat while we continued aimlessly to drift upon the face of the waters. It was now five o'clock, and the fog had so far lightened that we could see each other and a stretch of open water. At intervals the fog-horns of vessels passing us, but hidden from us, tormented Aldrich to a state of extreme exasperation. He hailed them with frantic shrieks and shouts, and Stumps and the Lady Moya shouted with him. I fear Kinney and myself did not contribute any great volume of sound to the general chorus. To be "rescued" was the last thing we desired. The yacht or tug that would receive us on board would also put us on shore, where the vindictive Aldrich would have us at his mercy. We preferred the freedom of our yawl and the shelter of the fog. Our silence was not lost upon Aldrich. For some time he had been crouching in the bow, whispering indignantly to Lady Moya; now he exclaimed aloud:

"What did I tell you?" he cried contemptuously; "they got away in this boat because they were afraid of *me*, not because they were afraid of being drowned. If they've nothing to be afraid of, why are they so anxious to keep us drifting around all night in this fog? Why don't they help us stop one of those tugs?"

Lord Ivy exploded suddenly.

"Rot!" he exclaimed. "If they're afraid of you, why did they ask you to go with them?"

"They didn't!" cried Aldrich, truthfully and triumphantly. "They kidnapped you and Moya because they thought they could square themselves with *you*. But they didn't want *me!*" The issue had been fairly stated, and no longer with self-respect could I remain silent.

"We don't want you now!" I said. "Can't you understand," I went on with as much self-restraint as I could muster, "we are willing and anxious to explain ourselves to Lord Ivy, or even to you, but we don't want to explain to the police? My friend thought you and Lord Ivy were crooks, escaping. You think *we* are crooks, escaping. You both——"

Aldrich snorted contemptuously.

"That's a likely story!" he cried. "No wonder you don't want to tell *that* to the police!"

From the bow came an exclamation, and Lady Moya rose to her feet.

"Phil!" she said, "you bore me!" She picked her way across the thwart to where Kinney sat at the stroke oar.

"My brother and I often row together," she said; "I will take your place."

When she had seated herself we were so near that her eyes looked directly into mine. Drawing in the oars, she leaned upon them and smiled.

"Now, then," she commanded, "tell us all about it."

Before I could speak there came from behind her a sudden radiance, and as though a curtain had been snatched aside, the fog flew apart, and the sun, dripping, crimson, and gorgeous, sprang from the waters. From the others there was a cry of wonder and delight, and from Lord Ivy a shriek of incredulous laughter.

Lady Moya clapped her hands joyfully and pointed past me. I turned and looked. Directly behind me, not fifty feet from us, was a shelving beach and a stone wharf, and above it a vine-covered cottage, from the chimney of which smoke curled cheerily. Had the yawl, while Lady Moya was taking the oars, *not* swung in a circle, and had the sun *not* risen, in three minutes more we would have bumped ourselves into the State of Connecticut. The cottage stood on one horn of a tiny harbor. Beyond it, weather-beaten, shingled houses, sail-lofts, and wharfs stretched cosily in a half-circle. Back of them rose splendid elms and the delicate spire of a church, and from the unruffled surface of the harbor the masts of many fishing-boats. Across the water, on a grass-grown point, a whitewashed light-house blushed in the crimson glory of the sun. Except for an oysterman in his boat at the end of the wharf, and the smoke from the chimney of his cottage, the little village slept, the harbor slept. It was a picture of perfect content, confidence, and peace. "Oh!" cried the Lady Moya, "how pretty, how pretty!"

Lord Ivy swung the bow about and raced toward the wharf. The others stood up and cheered hysterically.

At the sound and at the sight of us emerging so mysteriously from the fog, the man in the fishing-boat raised himself to his full height and stared as incredulously as though he beheld a mermaid. He was an old man, but straight and tall, and the oysterman's boots stretching to his hips made him appear even taller than he was. He had a bristling white beard and his face was tanned to a fierce copper color, but his eyes were blue and young and gentle. They lit suddenly with excitement and sympathy.

"Are you from the *Patience?*" he shouted. In chorus we answered that we were, and Ivy pulled the yawl alongside the fisherman's boat.

But already the old man had turned and, making a megaphone of his hands, was shouting to the cottage.

"Mother!" he cried, "mother, here are folks

from the wreck. Get coffee and blankets and—
and bacon—and eggs!"

"May the Lord bless him!" exclaimed the
Lady Moya devoutly.

But Aldrich, excited and eager, pulled out a
roll of bills and shook them at the man.

"Do you want to earn ten dollars?" he demanded; "then chase yourself to the village
and bring the constable."

Lady Moya exclaimed bitterly, Lord Ivy
swore, Kinney in despair uttered a dismal howl
and dropped his head in his hands.

"It's no use, Mr. Aldrich," I said. Seated in
the stern, the others had hidden me from the
fisherman. Now I stood up and he saw me.
I laid one hand on his, and pointed to the tin
badge on his suspender.

"He is the village constable himself," I explained. I turned to the lovely lady. "Lady
Moya," I said, "I want to introduce you to my
father!" I pointed to the vine-covered cottage.
"That's my home," I said. I pointed to the
sleeping town. "That," I told her, "is the
village of Fairport. Most of it belongs to
father. You are all very welcome."

# PEACE MANŒUVRES

THE scout stood where three roads cut three green tunnels in the pine woods, and met at his feet. Above his head an aged sign-post pointed impartially to East Carver, South Carver, and Carver Centre, and left the choice to him.

The scout scowled and bit nervously at his gauntlet. The choice was difficult, and there was no one with whom he could take counsel. The three sun-shot roads lay empty, and the other scouts, who, with him, had left the main column at sunrise, he had ordered back. They were to report that on the right flank, so far, at least, as Middleboro, there was no sign of the enemy. What lay beyond, it now was his duty to discover. The three empty roads spread before him like a picture-puzzle, smiling at his predicament. Whichever one he followed left two unguarded. Should he creep upon for choice Carver Centre, the enemy, masked by a mile of fir-trees, might advance from Carver or South Carver, and obviously he could not follow three roads at the same time. He considered the better strategy would be to wait where he was, where the three roads met, and allow the enemy himself to disclose his position. To the scout this course was most distasteful. He assured himself that this was so because, while it were the safer course, it wasted time and lacked initiative. But in his heart he knew that was not the reason, and to his heart his head answered that when one's country is at war, when fields and firesides are trampled by the iron heels of the invader, a scout should act not according to the dictates of his heart, but in the service of his native land. In the case of this particular patriot, the man and scout were at odds. As one of the Bicycle Squad of the Boston Corps of Cadets, the scout knew what, at this momentous crisis in her history, the commonwealth of Massachusetts demanded of him. It was that he sit tight and wait for the hated foreigners from New York City, New Jersey, and Connecticut to show themselves. But the man knew, and had known for several years, that on the road to Carver was the summer home of one Beatrice Farrar. As Private Lathrop it was no part of his duty to know that. As a man and a lover, and a rejected lover at that, he could not think of anything else. Struggling between love and duty the scout basely decided to leave the momentous question to chance. In the front tire of his bicycle was a puncture, temporarily effaced by a plug. Laying the bicycle on the ground, Lathrop spun the front wheel swiftly.

"If," he decided, "the wheel stops with the puncture pointing at Carver Centre, I'll advance upon Carver Centre. Should it point to either of the two other villages, I'll stop here.

"It's a two-to-one shot against me, anyway," he growled.

Kneeling in the road he spun the wheel, and as intently as at Monte Carlo and Palm Beach he had waited for other wheels to determine his fortune, he watched it come to rest. It stopped with the plug pointing back to Middleboro.

The scout told himself he was entitled to another trial. Again he spun the wheel. Again the spokes flashed in the sun. Again the puncture rested on the road to Middleboro.

"If it does that once more," thought the scout, "it's a warning that there is trouble ahead for me at Carver, and all the little Carvers."

For the third time the wheel flashed, but as he waited for the impetus to die, the sound of galloping hoofs broke sharply on the silence. The scout threw himself and his bicycle over the nearest stone wall, and, unlimbering his rifle, pointed it down the road.

He saw approaching a small boy, in a white apron, seated in a white wagon, on which was

painted, "Pies and Pastry. East Wareham."
The boy dragged his horse to an abrupt
halt.

"Don't point that at me!" shouted the boy.

"Where do you come from?" demanded the
scout.

"Wareham," said the baker.

"Are you carrying any one concealed in that
wagon?"

As though to make sure the baker's boy
glanced apprehensively into the depths of his
cart, and then answered that in the wagon he
carried nothing but fresh-baked bread. To
the trained nostrils of the scout this already was
evident. Before sunrise he had breakfasted on
hard tack and muddy coffee, and the odor of
crullers and mince pie, still warm, assailed him
cruelly. He assumed a fierce and terrible
aspect.

"Where are you going?" he challenged.

"To Carver Centre," said the boy.

To chance Lathrop had left the decision. He
believed the fates had answered.

Dragging his bicycle over the stone wall, he
fell into the road.

"Go on," he commanded. "I'll use your
cart for a screen. I'll creep behind the enemy
before he sees me."

The baker's boy frowned unhappily.

"But supposing," he argued, "they see you first, will they shoot?"

The scout waved his hand carelessly.

"Of course," he cried.

"Then," said the baker, "my horse will run away!"

"What of it?" demanded the scout. "Are Middleboro, South Middleboro, Rock, Brockton, and Boston to fall? Are they to be captured because you're afraid of your own horse? They won't shoot *real* bullets. This is not a real war. Don't you know that?"

The baker's boy flushed with indignation.

"Sure, I know that," he protested; "but my horse—*he* don't know that!"

Lathrop slung his rifle over his shoulder and his leg over his bicycle.

"If the Reds catch you," he warned, in parting, "they'll take everything you've got."

"The Blues have took most of it already," wailed the boy. "And just as they were paying me the battle begun, and this horse run away, and I couldn't get him to come back for my money."

"War," exclaimed Lathrop morosely, "is always cruel to the innocent." He sped toward Carver Centre. In his motor car, he had travelled the road many times, and as always his goal had been the home of Miss Beatrice Farrar,

he had covered it at a speed unrecognized by
law. But now he advanced with stealth and
caution. In every clump of bushes he saw an
ambush. Behind each rock he beheld the
enemy.

In a clearing was a group of Portuguese cran-
berry pickers, dressed as though for a holiday.
When they saw the man in uniform, one of the
women hailed him anxiously.

"Is the parade coming?" she called.

"Have you seen any of the Reds?" Lathrop
returned.

"No," complained the woman. "And we
been waiting all morning. When will the parade
come?"

"It's not a parade," said Lathrop, severely.
"It's a war!"

The summer home of Miss Farrar stood close
to the road. It had been so placed by the farmer
who built it, in order that the women folk might
sit at the window and watch the passing of the
stage-coach and the peddler. Great elms hung
over it, and a white fence separated the road
from the narrow lawn. At a distance of a hundred yards a turn brought the house into view,
and at this turn, as had been his manœuvre at
every other possible ambush, Lathrop dismounted and advanced on foot. Up to this
moment the road had been empty, but now,

in front of the Farrar cottage, it was blocked by a touring-car and a station wagon. In the occupants of the car he recognized all the members of the Farrar family, except Miss Farrar. In the station wagon were all of the Farrar servants. Miss Farrar herself was leaning upon the gate and waving them a farewell. The touring-car moved off down the road; the station wagon followed; Miss Farrar was alone. Lathrop scorched toward her, and when he was opposite the gate, dug his toes in the dust and halted. When he lifted his broad-brimmed campaign hat, Miss Farrar exclaimed both with surprise and displeasure. Drawing back from the gate she held herself erect. Her attitude was that of one prepared for instant retreat. When she spoke it was in tones of extreme disapproval.

"You promised," said the girl, "you would not come to see me."

Lathrop, straddling his bicycle, peered anxiously down the road.

"This is not a social call," he said. "I'm on duty. Have you seen the Reds?"

His tone was brisk and alert, his manner preoccupied. The ungraciousness of his reception did not seem in the least to disconcert him.

But Miss Farrar was not deceived. She knew him, not only as a persistent and irrepressible lover, but as one full of guile, adroit in tricks, fertile in expedients. He was one who could not take "No" for an answer—at least not from her. When she repulsed him she seemed to grow in his eyes only the more attractive.

"It is not the lover who comes to woo," he was constantly explaining, "but the lover's *way* of wooing."

Miss Farrar had assured him she did not like his way. She objected to being regarded and treated as a castle that could be taken only by assault. Whether she wished time to consider, or whether he and his proposal were really obnoxious to her, he could not find out. His policy of campaign was that she, also, should not have time to find out. Again and again she had agreed to see him only on the condition that he would not make love to her. He had promised again and again, and had failed to keep that promise. Only a week before he had been banished from her presence, to remain an exile until she gave him permission to see her at her home in New York. It was not her purpose to return there for two weeks, and yet here he was, a beggar at her gate. It might be that he was there, as he said, "on duty," but her knowledge of him and of the doctrine of chances caused her to doubt it.

"Mr. Lathrop!" she began, severely.

As though to see to whom she had spoken Lathrop glanced anxiously over his shoulder. Apparently pained and surprised to find that it was to him she had addressed herself, he regarded her with deep reproach. His eyes were very beautiful. It was a fact which had often caused Miss Farrar extreme annoyance.

He shook his head sadly.

"'Mr. Lathrop?'" he protested. "You know that to you I am always 'Charles—Charles the Bold,' because I am bold to love you; but never 'Mr. Lathrop,' unless," he went on briskly, "you are referring to a future state, when, as Mrs. Lathrop, you will make me——"

Miss Farrar had turned her back on him, and was walking rapidly up the path.

"Beatrice," he called. "I am coming after you!"

Miss Farrar instantly returned and placed both hands firmly upon the gate.

"I cannot understand you!" she said. "Don't you see that when you act as you do now, I can't even respect you? How do you think I could ever care, when you offend me so? You jest at what you pretend is the most serious thing in your life. You play with it—laugh at it!"

The young man interrupted her sharply.

"It's like this," he said. "When I am with you I am so happy I can't be serious. When I am *not* with you, it is *so* serious that I am utterly and completely wretched. You say my love offends you, bores you! I am sorry, but what, in heaven's name, do you think your *not* loving me is doing to *me?* I am a wreck! I am a skeleton! Look at me!"

He let his bicycle fall, and stood with his hands open at his sides, as though inviting her to gaze upon the ruin she had caused.

Four days of sun and rain, astride of a bicycle, without food or sleep, had drawn his face into fine, hard lines, had bronzed it with a healthy tan. His uniform, made by the same tailor that fitted him with polo breeches, clung to him like a jersey. The spectacle he presented was that of an extremely picturesque, handsome, manly youth, and of that fact no one was better aware than himself.

"Look at me," he begged, sadly.

Miss Farrar was entirely unimpressed.

"I am!" she returned, coldly. "I never saw you looking so well—and you know it." She gave a gasp of comprehension. "You came here because you knew your uniform was becoming!"

Lathrop regarded himself complacently.

"Yes, isn't it?" he assented. "I brought on

this war in order to wear it. If you don't mind," he added, "I think I'll accept your invitation and come inside. I've had nothing to eat in four days."

Miss Farrar's eyes flashed indignantly.

"You're *not* coming inside," she declared; "but if you'll only promise to go away at once, I'll bring you everything in the house."

"In that house," exclaimed Lathrop, dramatically, "there's only one thing that I desire, and I want that so badly that 'life holds no charm without you.'"

Miss Farrar regarded him steadily.

"Do you intend to drive me away from my own door, or will you go?"

Lathrop picked his wheel out of the dust.

"Good-by," he said. "I'll come back when you have made up your mind."

In vexation Miss Farrar stamped her foot upon the path.

"I *have* made up my mind!" she protested.

"Then," returned Lathrop, "I'll come back when you have changed it."

He made a movement as though to ride away, but much to Miss Farrar's dismay, hastily dismounted. "On second thoughts," he said, "it isn't right for me to leave you. The woods are full of tramps and hangers-on of the army. You're not safe. I can watch this road from here as well as from anywhere else, and at the same time I can guard you."

To the consternation of Miss Farrar he placed his bicycle against the fence, and, as though preparing for a visit, leaned his elbows upon it.

"I do not wish to be rude," said Miss Farrar, "but you are annoying me. I have spent fifteen summers in Massachusetts, and I have never seen a tramp. I need no one to guard me."

"If not you," said Lathrop easily, "then the family silver. And think of your jewels, and your mother's jewels. Think of yourself in a house filled with jewels, and entirely surrounded by hostile armies! My duty is to remain with you."

Miss Farrar was so long in answering, that Lathrop lifted his head and turned to look. He found her frowning and gazing intently into the shadow of the woods, across the road. When she felt his eyes upon her she turned her own guiltily upon him. Her cheeks were flushed and her face glowed with some unusual excitement.

"I wish," she exclaimed breathlessly—"I wish," she repeated, "the Reds would take you prisoner!"

"Take me where?" asked Lathrop.

"Take you anywhere!" cried Miss Farrar. "You should be ashamed to talk to me when you should be looking for the enemy!"

"I am *waiting* for the enemy," explained Lathrop. "It's the same thing."

Miss Farrar smiled vindictively. Her eyes shone.

"You need not wait long," she said.

There was a crash of a falling stone wall, and of parting bushes, but not in time to give Lathrop warning. As though from the branches of the trees opposite two soldiers fell into the road; around his hat each wore the red band of the invader; each pointed his rifle at Lathrop.

"Hands up!" shouted one. "You're my prisoner!" cried the other.

Mechanically Lathrop raised his hands, but his eyes turned to Miss Farrar.

"Did you know?" he asked.

"I have been watching them," she said, "creeping up on you for the last ten minutes."

Lathrop turned to the two soldiers, and made an effort to smile.

"That was very clever," he said, "but I have twenty men up the road, and behind them a regiment. You had better get away while you can."

The two Reds laughed derisively. One, who wore the stripes of a sergeant, answered: "That won't do! We been a mile up the road, and you and us are the only soldiers on it. Gimme the gun!"

Lathrop knew he had no right to refuse. He

had been fairly surprised, but he hesitated. When Miss Farrar was not in his mind his amateur soldiering was to him a most serious proposition. The war game was a serious proposition, and that, through his failure for ten minutes to regard it seriously, he had been made a prisoner, mortified him keenly. That his humiliation had taken place in the presence of Beatrice Farrar did not lessen his discomfort, nor did the explanation he must later make to his captain afford him any satisfaction. Already he saw himself playing the star part in a court-martial. He shrugged his shoulders and surrendered his gun.

As he did so he gloomily scrutinized the insignia of his captors.

"Who took me?" he asked.

"*We* took you," exclaimed the sergeant.

"What regiment?" demanded Lathrop, sharply. "I have to report who took me; and you probably don't know it, but your collar ornaments are upside down." With genuine exasperation he turned to Miss Farrar.

"Lord!" he exclaimed, "isn't it bad enough to be taken prisoner, without being taken by raw recruits that can't put on their uniforms?"

The Reds flushed, and the younger, a sandy-haired, rat-faced youth, retorted angrily: "Mebbe we ain't strong on uniforms, beau," he snarled, "but you've got nothing on us yet, that I can see. You look pretty with your hands in the air, don't you?"

"Shut up," commanded the other Red. He was the older man, heavily built, with a strong, hard mouth and chin, on which latter sprouted a three days' iron-gray beard. "Don't you see he's an officer? Officers don't like being took by two-spot privates."

Lathrop gave a sudden start. "Why," he laughed, incredulously, "don't you know—" He stopped, and his eyes glanced quickly up and down the road.

"Don't we know what?" demanded the older Red, suspiciously.

"I forgot," said Lathrop. "I—I must not give information to the enemy—"

For an instant there was a pause, while the two Reds stood irresolute. Then the older nodded the other to the side of the road, and in whispers they consulted eagerly.

Miss Farrar laughed, and Lathrop moved toward her.

"I deserve worse than being laughed at," he said. "I made a strategic mistake. I should not have tried to capture you and an army corps at the same time."

"You," she taunted, "who were always so keen on soldiering, to be taken prisoner," she lowered her voice, "and by men like that! Aren't they funny?" she whispered, "and East Side and Tenderloin! It made me homesick to hear them! I think when not in uniform the little one drives a taxicab, and the big one is a guard on the elevated."

"They certainly are very 'New York,'" assented Lathrop, "and very tough."

"I thought," whispered Miss Farrar, "those from New York with the Red Army were picked men."

"What does it matter?" exclaimed Lathrop. "It's just as humiliating to be captured by a hall-room boy as by a mere millionaire! I can't insist on the invading army being entirely recruited from Harvard graduates."

The two Reds either had reached a decision or agreed that they could not agree, for they ceased whispering, and crossed to where Lathrop stood.

"We been talking over your case," explained the sergeant, "and we see we are in wrong. We see we made a mistake in taking you prisoner. We had ought to shot you dead. So now we're going to shoot you dead."

"You can't!" objected Lathrop. "It's too late. You should have thought of that sooner."

"I know," admitted the sergeant, "but a prisoner is a hell of a nuisance. If you got a prisoner to look after you can't do your own work; you got to keep tabs on him. And there ain't nothing in it for the prisoner, neither. If we take you, you'll have to tramp all the way to our army, and all the way back. But, if you're dead, how different! You ain't no bother to anybody. You got a half-holiday all to yourself, and you can loaf around the camp, so dead that they can't make you work, but not so dead you can't smoke or eat." The sergeant smiled ingratiatingly. In a tempting manner he exhibited his rifle. "Better be dead," he urged.

"I'd like to oblige you," said Lathrop, "but it's against the rules. You *can't* shoot a prisoner."

The rat-faced soldier uttered an angry exclamation. "To hell with the rules!" he cried. "We can't waste time on him. Turn him loose!"

The older man rounded on the little one savagely. The tone in which he addressed him was cold, menacing, sinister. His words were simple, but his eyes and face were heavy with warning.

"Who is running this?" he asked.

The little soldier muttered, and shuffled away. From under the brim of his campaign hat, his eyes cast furtive glances up and down the road.

As though anxious to wipe out the effect of his comrade's words, the sergeant addressed Lathrop suavely and in a tone of conciliation.

"You see," he explained, "him and me are scouts. We're not supposed to waste time taking prisoners. So, we'll set you free." He waved his hand invitingly toward the bicycle. "You can go!" he said.

To Miss Farrar's indignation Lathrop, instead of accepting his freedom, remained motionless.

"I can't!" he said. "I'm on post. My captain ordered me to stay in front of this house until I was relieved."

Miss Farrar, amazed at such duplicity, exclaimed aloud:

"He is *not* on post!" she protested. "He's a scout! He wants to stop here, because—because —he's hungry. I wouldn't have let you take him prisoner, if I had not thought you would take him away with you." She appealed to the sergeant. "*Please* take him away," she begged.

The sergeant turned sharply upon his prisoner.

"Why don't you do what the lady wants?" he demanded.

"Because I've got to do what my captain wants," returned Lathrop, "and he put me on sentry-go, in front of this house."

With the back of his hand, the sergeant fretfully scraped the three days' growth on his chin.

"There's nothing to it," he exclaimed, "but for to take him with us. When we meet some more Reds we'll turn him over. Fall in!" he commanded.

"No!" protested Lathrop. "I don't want to be turned over. I've got a much better plan. *You* don't want to be bothered with a prisoner. *I* don't want to be a prisoner. As you say, I am better dead. You can't shoot a prisoner, but if he tries to escape you can. I'll try to escape. You shoot me. Then I return to my own army, and report myself dead. That ends your difficulty and saves me from a court-martial. They can't court-martial a corpse."

The face of the sergeant flashed with relief and satisfaction. In his anxiety to rid himself of his prisoner, he lifted the bicycle into the road and held it in readiness.

"You're all right!" he said, heartily. "You can make your getaway as quick as you like."

But to the conspiracy Miss Farrar refused to lend herself.

"How do you know," she demanded, "that he will keep his promise? He may not go back to his own army. He can be just as dead on my lawn as anywhere else!"

Lathrop shook his head at her sadly.

"How you wrong me!" he protested. "How dare you doubt the promise of a dying man?

These are really my last words, and I wish I could think of something to say suited to the occasion, but the presence of strangers prevents."

He mounted his bicycle. "'If I had a thousand lives to give,'" he quoted with fervor, "'I'd give them all to—'" he hesitated, and smiled mournfully on Miss Farrar. Seeing her flushed and indignant countenance, he added, with haste, "to the Commonwealth of Massachusetts!"

As he started on his wheel slowly down the path, he turned to the sergeant.

"I'm escaping," he explained. The Reds, with an enthusiasm undoubtedly genuine, raised their rifles, and the calm of the Indian summer was shattered by two sharp reports. Lathrop, looking back over his shoulder, waved one hand reassuringly.

"Death was instantaneous," he called. He bent his body over the handle-bar, and they watched him disappear rapidly around the turn in the road.

Miss Farrar sighed with relief.

"Thank you very much," he said.

As though signifying that to oblige a woman he would shoot any number of prisoners, the sergeant raised his hat.

"Don't mention it, lady," he said. "I seen he was annoying you, and that's why I got rid of him. Some of them amateur soldiers, as soon as they get into uniform, are too fresh. He took advantage of you because your folks were away from home. But don't you worry about that. I'll guard this house until your folks get back."

Miss Farrar protested warmly.

"Really!" she exclaimed; "I need no one to guard me."

But the soldier was obdurate. He motioned his comrade down the road.

"Watch at the turn," he ordered; "he may come back or send some of the Blues to take us. I'll stay here and protect the lady."

Again Miss Farrar protested, but the sergeant, in a benign and fatherly manner, smiled approvingly. Seating himself on the grass outside the fence, he leaned his back against the gatepost, apparently settling himself for conversation.

"Now, how long might it have been," he asked, "before we showed up, that you seen us?"

"I saw you," Miss Farrar said, "when Mr.— when that bicycle scout was talking to me. I saw the red bands on your hats among the bushes."

The sergeant appeared interested.

"But why didn't you let on to him?"

Miss Farrar laughed evasively.

"Maybe because I am from New York, too," she said. "Perhaps I wanted to see soldiers from my city take a prisoner."

They were interrupted by the sudden appearance of the smaller soldier. On his rat-like countenance was written deep concern.

"When I got to the turn," he began, breathlessly, "I couldn't see him. Where did he go? Did he double-back through the woods, or did he have time to ride out of sight before I got there?"

The reappearance of his comrade affected the sergeant strangely. He sprang to his feet, his under jaw protruding truculently, his eyes flashing with anger.

"Get back," he snarled. "Do what I told you!"

Under his breath he muttered words that, to Miss Farrar, were unintelligible. The little rat-like man nodded, and ran from them down the road. The sergeant made an awkward gesture of apology.

"Excuse me, lady," he begged, "but it makes me hot when them rookies won't obey orders. You see," he ran on glibly, "I'm a reg'lar; served three years in the Philippines, and I can't get used to not having my men do what I say."

Miss Farrar nodded, and started toward the

house. The sergeant sprang quickly across the road.

"Have you ever been in the Philippines, Miss?" he called. "It's a great country."

Miss Farrar halted and shook her head. She was considering how far politeness required of her to entertain unshaven militiamen, who insisted on making sentries of themselves at her front gate.

The sergeant had plunged garrulously into a confusing description of the Far East. He was clasping the pickets of the fence with his hands, and his eyes were fastened on hers. He lacked neither confidence nor vocabulary, and not for an instant did his tongue hesitate or his eyes wander, and yet in his manner there was nothing at which she could take offense. He appeared only amiably vain that he had seen much of the world, and anxious to impress that fact upon another. Miss Farrar was bored, but the man gave her no opportunity to escape. In consequence she was relieved when the noisy approach of an automobile brought him to an abrupt pause. Coming rapidly down the road was a large touring-car, filled with men in khaki. The sergeant gave one glance at it, and leaped across the road, taking cover behind the stone wall. Instantly he raised his head above it and shook his fist at Miss Farrar.

"Don't tell," he commanded. "They're Blues in that car! Don't tell!" Again he sank from sight.

Miss Farrar now was more than bored, she was annoyed. Why grown men should play at war so seriously she could not understand. It was absurd! She no longer would remain a party to it; and, lest the men in the car might involve her still further, she retreated hastily toward the house. As she opened the door the car halted at the gate, and voices called to her, but she pretended not to hear them, and continued up the stairs. Behind her the car passed noisily on its way.

She mounted the stairs, and crossing a landing moved down a long hall, at the further end of which was her bedroom. The hall was uncarpeted, but the tennis shoes she wore made no sound, nor did the door of her bedroom when she pushed it open.

On the threshold Miss Farrar stood quite still. A swift, sinking nausea held her in a vise. Her instinct was to scream and run, but her throat had tightened and gone dry, and her limbs trembled. Opposite the door was her dressing-table, and reflected in its mirror were the features and figure of the rat-like soldier. His back was toward her. With one hand he swept the dressing-table. The other, hanging at his side, held a revolver. In a moment the panic into which Miss Farrar had been thrown passed. Her breath and blood returned, and, intent only on flight, she softly turned. On the instant the rat-faced one raised his eyes, saw her reflected in the mirror, and with an oath, swung toward her. He drew the revolver close to his cheek, and looked at her down the barrel. "Don't move!" he whispered; "don't scream! Where are the jewels?"

Miss Farrar was not afraid of the revolver or of the man. She did not believe either would do her harm. The idea of both the presence of the man in her room, and that any one should dare to threaten her was what filled her with repugnance. As the warm blood flowed again through her body her spirit returned. She was no longer afraid. She was, instead, indignant, furious.

With one step she was in the room, leaving the road to the door open.

"Get out of here," she commanded.

The little man snarled, and stamped the floor. He shoved the gun nearer to her.

"The jewels, damn you!" he whispered. "Do you want me to blow your fool head off? Where are the jewels?"

"Jewels?" repeated Miss Farrar. "I have no jewels!"

"You lie!" shrieked the little man. "He said the house was full of jewels. We heard him. He said he would stay to guard the jewels."

Miss Farrar recognized his error. She remembered Lathrop's jest, and that it had been made while the two men were within hearing, behind the stone wall.

"It was a joke!" she cried. "Leave at once!" She backed swiftly toward the open window that looked upon the road. "Or I'll call your sergeant!"

"If you go near that window or scream," whispered the rat-like one, "I'll shoot!"

A heavy voice, speaking suddenly from the doorway, shook Miss Farrar's jangled nerves into fresh panic.

"She won't scream," said the voice.

In the door Miss Farrar saw the bulky form of the sergeant, blocking her escape.

Without shifting his eyes from Miss Farrar, the man with the gun cursed breathlessly at the other. "Why didn't you keep her away?" he panted.

"An automobile stopped in front of the gate," explained the sergeant. "Have you got them?" he demanded.

"No!" returned the other. "Nothing! She won't tell where they are."

The older man laughed. "Oh, yes, she'll tell," he whispered. His voice was still low and suave, but it carried with it the weight of a threat, and the threat, although unspoken, filled Miss Farrar with alarm. Her eyes, wide with concern, turned fearfully from one man to the other.

The sergeant stretched his hands toward her, the fingers working and making clutches in the air. The look in his eyes was quite terrifying. "If you don't tell," he said slowly, "I'll choke it out of you!"

If his intention was to frighten the girl, he succeeded admirably. With her hands clasped to her throat, Miss Farrar sank against the wall. She saw no chance of escape. The way to the door was barred, and should she drop to the garden below, from the window, before she could reach the road the men would overtake her. Even should she reach the road, the house nearest was a half-mile distant.

The sergeant came close, his fingers opening and closing in front of her eyes. He raised his voice to a harsh, bellowing roar. "I'm going to make you tell!" he shouted. "I'm going to choke it out of you!"

Although she was alone in the house, although on every side the pine woods encompassed her, Miss Farrar threw all her strength into one long, piercing cry for help. And upon the instant it was answered. From the hall came the swift rush of feet. The rat-like one swung toward it. From his revolver came a report that shook the room, a flash and a burst of smoke, and through it Miss Farrar saw Lathrop hurl himself. He dived at the rat-like one, and as on the foot-ball field he had been taught to stop a runner, flung his arms around the other's knees. The legs of the man shot from under him, his body cut a half-circle through the air, and the part of his anatomy to first touch the floor was his head. The floor was of oak, and the impact gave forth a crash like the smash of a base-ball bat, when it drives the ball to centre field. The man did not move. He did not even groan. In his relaxed fingers the revolver lay, within reach of Lathrop's hand. He fell upon it and, still on his knees, pointed it at the sergeant.

"You're *my* prisoner, now!" he shouted cheerfully. "Hands up!"

The man raised his arms slowly, as if he were lifting heavy dumb-bells.

"The lady called for help," he said. "I came to help her."

"No! No!" protested the girl. "He did *not* help me! He said he would choke me if I didn't——"

"He said he would—what!" bellowed La-

303

throp. He leaped to his feet, and sent the gun spinning through the window. He stepped toward the man gingerly, on the balls of his feet, like one walking on ice. The man seemed to know what that form of approach threatened, for he threw his arms into a position of defense.

"You bully!" whispered Lathrop. "You coward! You choke women, do you?"

He shifted from one foot to the other, his body balancing forward, his arms swinging limply in front of him. With his eyes, he seemed to undress the man, as thcugh choosing a place to strike.

"I made the same mistake you did," he taunted. "I should have killed you first. Now I am going to do it!"

He sprang at the man, his chin still sunk on his chest, but with his arms swinging like the spokes of a wheel. His opponent struck back heavily, violently, but each move of his arm seemed only to open up some vulnerable spot. Blows beat upon his chin, upon his nose, his eyes; blows jabbed him in the ribs, drove his breath from his stomach, ground his teeth together, cut the flesh from his cheeks. He sank to his knees, with his arms clasping his head.

"Get up!" roared Lathrop. "Stand up to it, you coward!"

But the man had no idea of standing up to it. Howling with pain, he scrambled toward the door, and fled staggering down the hall.

At the same moment the automobile that a few minutes before had passed up the road came limping to the gate, and a half-dozen men in uniform sprang out of it. From the window Lathrop saw them spread across the lawn and surround the house.

"They've got him!" he said. He pointed to the prostrate figure on the floor. "He and the other one," he explained, breathlessly, "are New York crooks! They have been looting in the wake of the Reds, disguised as soldiers. I knew they weren't even amateur soldiers by the mistakes in their make-up, and I made that bluff of riding away so as to give them time to show what the game was. Then, that provost guard in the motor car stopped me, and when they said who they were after, I ordered them back here. But they had a flat tire, and my bicycle beat them."

In his excitement he did not notice that the girl was not listening, that she was very pale, that she was breathing quickly, and trembling.

"I'll go tell them," he added, "that the other one they want is up here."

Miss Farrar's strength instantly returned.

With a look of terror at the now groaning

figure on the floor, she sprang toward Lathrop, with both hands clutching him by his sleeves.

"You will *not!*" she commanded. "You will not leave me alone!"

Appealingly she raised her face to his startled countenance. With a burst of tears she threw herself into his arms. "I'm afraid!" she sobbed. "Don't leave me. Please, no matter what I say, never leave me again!"

Between bewilderment and joy, the face of Lathrop was unrecognizable. As her words reached him, as he felt the touch of her body in his arms, and her warm, wet cheek against his own, he drew a deep sigh of content, and then, fearfully and tenderly, held her close.

After a pause, in which peace came to all the world, he raised his head.

"Don't worry!" he said. "You can *bet* I won't leave you!"